W9-BSR-789

Beyond the Attractions:
A **Guide** to **Walt Disney World** with **Preschoolers**
(2012)

Lisa M. Battista

CreateSpace

MRB Ventures, LLC Book Notice and Disclaimer

1. COPYRIGHT NOTICE: Copyright © 2011 MRB Ventures, LLC (MRB). ALL RIGHTS RESERVED UNDER UNITED STATES OF AMERICA AND INTERNATIONAL COPYRIGHT LAWS. NO PART OF THIS BOOK PUBLICATION MAY BE REPRODUCED, STORED ON ELECTRONIC MEDIA, OR TRANSMITTED IN ANY FORM OR BY ANY MEANS WHETHER ELECTRONIC, MECHANICAL, PHOTOCOPY, RECORDING, OR OTHERWISE WITHOUT THE EXPRESS WRITTEN PERMISSION OF MRB, LLC.

2. CONTENT DISCLAIMER: MRB has made commercially reasonable efforts to ensure that the information contained in this book ("Book") is current. All information provided in this Book, and in particular, details such as website addresses, telephone numbers, attraction prices, operating hours, and the like, are liable to change. MRB cannot accept any responsibility or extend any warranty for the accuracy of such information or the information of referenced third party sources (e.g., websites), or for the consequences arising from any use of this Book. MRB carries no affiliation or association with, and expressly represents, notwithstanding any statement to the contrary herein, that it does NOT recommend any particular service, product, brand, venue, destination or like reference contained in this Book. For the avoidance of doubt, MRB has no affiliation, licensing relationship or other association with Walt Disney World, Walt Disney Parks and Resorts, LLC, Disney Enterprises, Inc., or any of their respective subsidiaries, affiliated, and related companies.

Copyright © 2011 MRB Ventures, LLC. All rights reserved.
www.beyondtheattractions.com

ISBN-10: 1463791399
ISBN-13: 978-1463791391

PRINTED IN THE UNITED STATES OF AMERICA

For my boys, who are the greatest blessings in my life.

Acknowledgments

I am very fortunate to be part of a large and very warm community. Amanda Ficili, the Disney Go To Girl; Kelly Ortiz, the Disney Guru; and Lynn Wiltse of My Pixie Dust Diary volunteered their time to read the book and shared their Disney expertise to improve and tweak the 2012 edition of *Beyond the Attractions: A Guide to Walt Disney World with Preschoolers*.

Many thanks to Natalie Henley of Meet the Magic, and Lynn Wiltse of My Pixie Dust Diary who did some on the ground research for the book.

Beyond the Attractions wouldn't be what it is without the steady and expert guidance of my editor, Beverly Ehrman.

CONTENTS

CONTENTS

CONTENTS

CONTENTS

CONTENTS

Introduction

There's no point to taking kids under five to Disney World – they won't remember it anyway.

You've probably heard this sentiment before and maybe even had the same thought. I have to admit that I was a member of the "no-Disney-before-age-five" club for a time. But something changed on an adults-only Walt Disney World vacation when our son was one. My husband and I looked around and saw Walt Disney World through the eyes of new parents; there is so much more to Walt Disney World than attractions. In addition to the many rides our little guy could experience, we knew our curious son, who loved visual surprise and music, would delight in the abundance of one-of-a-kind cheerful sights and sounds at Walt Disney World. We realized we wanted to share that experience with him sooner rather than later.

As the mother of three, including a young adult stepson, I've observed every stage of childhood on many Walt Disney World vacations – baby, toddler, preschooler, pre-teen, teen, and young adult. I know there will be some additional challenges (do I have to say potty training) with preschoolers but their boundless ability to just believe in the magic makes the memories we create with them extra-special. When my youngest son is thirty, he may very well not remember much about the trip he took when he was two, but his father and I certainly will. I can, however, say with certainty that he does remember the trip now, months after we have returned. All he has to hear are those two words,

"Disney World" and a broad smile lights up his face while he frantically points to his nose – his sign for "Mickey Mouse."

If you are reading this book, you've most likely already decided to take your little ones to Walt Disney World. Perhaps you can't wait to see them wear their first pair of Mickey ears or maybe they're the youngest in the family and you don't want to put off a Walt Disney World trip for their brothers and sisters any longer. Whatever the reason, I can assure you that you can have a magical and memorable (in a good way!) Walt Disney World vacation with preschoolers.

Beyond the Attractions: A Guide to Walt Disney World with Preschoolers is written for parents, grandparents, aunts, uncles, and anyone who wants to share the magic of the Walt Disney World Resort with their preschoolers. The specialized information, tips, and insights will help you experience an unforgettable, fun-filled vacation with your little ones.

I sincerely hope this guide helps to make your preschooler's Walt Disney World trip as enchanting as our trips have been. There is nothing like experiencing your children's wide-eyed wonder as they take in the sights and sounds of Disney World.

For a list of changes to the Walt Disney World theme parks that have occurred since the printing of this book, visit www.BeyondTheAttractions.com. For more Disney news and views, follow @DisneyExplorer on Twitter and "like" the Beyond the Attractions Facebook page (www.facebook.com/BeyondtheAttractions). The author is not affiliated with the Walt Disney Company in any way.

A New Approach

This Walt Disney World guidebook differs from other Disney World guidebooks in that it is not a general overview of everything the parks have to offer – much of which may not apply to small children – but is devoted solely to visiting with preschoolers. With a Disney World travel guide that provides specialized information and tips relevant to small kids, you'll be able to plan an incredible trip with your preschoolers without wading through hundreds of pages of general information.

Notes. For ease of reading, the term parents will be used throughout the book to denote caregivers traveling with small children.

Walt Disney World has four theme parks and two water parks. The theme parks are Magic Kingdom®, Epcot®, Disney's Hollywood Studios™, and Animal Kingdom®. Water parks include Blizzard Beach and Typhoon Lagoon. This travel guide purposely does not cover the Walt Disney World water parks as they are more limited in the activities they offer preschoolers. Downtown Disney offers a wide variety of shopping and dining opportunities – best of all, entrance is free.

Disney prices are subject to change without notice. Every effort has been made to confirm current costs, which generally do not include tax. Costs are included in this guide for informational and planning purposes but are not guaranteed.

Top Six Tips

Have a Plan. There are an incredible number of attractions and recreational activities available at the Walt Disney World Resort. Research the park attractions and jot down your family's must-sees. Download theme park maps and calendars to familiarize yourself with each park's layout and hours prior to your visit. The Disney theme parks may close up to three hours earlier in the off-season. Park hours will influence your touring plans and dining times. See "Resources" for website addresses.

 Touring Plans (www.touringplans.com) provides an online crowd calendar. The crowd calendar uses statistical data to predict how crowded the Disney World theme parks are expected to be on a given day. Recommendations on the best parks to visit and parks to avoid for a particular day are provided. The crowd predictions for the next 31 to 60 days are available to anyone. For calendars that predict crowds outside this range, you must be a subscriber.

FASTPASS®. Walt Disney World ticket holders may take advantage of FASTPASS, a means of bypassing the standby line for a much shorter FASTPASS queue. Using FASTPASS can dramatically decrease the time you spend in line and increase the number of attractions your family will enjoy. Refer to Chapter 4, "Touring," for more FASTPASS details.

Start Early. It's tempting to sleep in at Walt Disney World. After all, you are on vacation. It's important to know that crowds are lighter when the parks first open, and during the warmer times of the year the weather is more hospitable early in the day. Get an early start to minimize the amount of time you spend on lines. When the crowds become heavier and the weather warmer, take a break and return to your hotel for a swim and a nap.

 Rope drop is the ceremony that signals the official opening of each park. Disney World typically allows guests into its parks 20-30 minutes prior to rope drop.

During this time, guests pass through security and the ticket turnstiles. You may move through each park until a certain point and then wait for rope drop. To get a head start on the day, arrive before the park opens and enjoy the opening ceremony.

Make Advance Dining Reservations (ADRs). With the many table-service restaurants in Walt Disney World, it's difficult to imagine not getting a table at the restaurant of your choice on the day you wish to dine. However, this routinely happens with the large crowds visiting the resort. It is best to make your ADRs, guaranteeing a table, well in advance of your trip by calling 407-WDW-DINE or visiting www.disneyworld.com to make them online.

Ask a Cast Member. Walt Disney World staff, or Cast Members, have been trained to provide an exceptional level of service and to make your vacation even more magical. If you have any problems, concerns, or questions, do not hesitate to ask the nearest Cast Member for help.

Wear Comfortable Shoes. This may seem obvious but I cannot tell you the number of people I see in very stylish but impractical footwear. It's easy to underestimate the amount of walking you'll be doing at the theme parks. Walking 5-10 miles a day is not unusual when visiting the Walt Disney World Resort.

Top Six Tips for Travel with Preschoolers

Be Flexible. The single most important thing you can do to have a successful Walt Disney World trip with preschoolers is to have a plan, and then be willing to deviate from it. When the kids get hot, tired, or over-stimulated, slow down the pace of your touring, have a snack, or take a break in your resort room. Yes, you may miss the afternoon parade or the next showing of Festival of the Lion King but the whole family will be happier if your little ones are content. On the other hand, your kids may surprise you and be able to tour longer than you thought.

Use a Stroller. Visiting Disney World is not like a typical day at your park or local zoo. Chances are you'll be out of your resort room for hours at a time and your family will put in mile after mile at the theme parks and at your resort. Even the most energetic four- or five-year-old who would never consider sitting in a stroller at home will likely be asking for one by midday. See Chapter 4, "Touring," for more information.

Don't Force the Issue. Preschoolers are a funny bunch. They sometimes have difficulty communicating a fear or just plain discomfort with a ride or situation. If they resist a particular attraction, don't force the issue; it's easier to find a ride they do enjoy than having to coax them on future rides if they have a "bad" experience. See Chapter 5, "Attractions," for a list of attractions that may scare little ones.

Ship Bulky Items. Times have changed and airlines charging their customers for each checked bag are becoming the norm. Travel with toddlers includes lots of bulky items such as diapers, wipes, sippy cups, and toddler utensils. If you need to bring disposable items, ship them to your Disney resort. The shipping costs will likely be less than baggage fees for a round-trip flight and you'll have less baggage to juggle to and from the airport. See Chapter 1, "Preparing," for more information.

Pack Snacks. There's no doubt about it, you may very well suffer from sticker shock at the Disney World snack locations. Pack some healthy dry snacks and water in your theme park bag.

A little pick-me-up may be just the thing for your child. You won't have to worry about a sugar high or your child not eating the next meal because of the super-sized park snacks.

Try a Lanyard. When at the parks, I try to travel light. My husband and I switch off carrying the backpack we bring to the park and sometimes divide and conquer the attractions and food; this means I cannot rely on putting my park pass, room key, FASTPASS, PhotoPass card, credit card, I.D., and a little bit of cash into the backpack. I've found the easiest way for me to carry all my cards is using a lanyard with an attached card-holder. I throw it around my neck and go. Mine was purchased at the local Walmart.

1   Preparing

With four theme parks, two water parks, Downtown Disney, a multitude of resorts and restaurants to choose from, and other recreational activities spread over many square miles, advance planning for your trip is critical. Going so far as to schedule your trip down to the minute with military precision probably won't result in the relaxed, memorable trip you want for your young family. Spending time familiarizing yourself with the layout of the parks, the attractions, and some key lodging and dining options will make your trip more relaxed and successful.

The Disney "Experience"

A Walt Disney World trip is far more than a vacation; it is an experience and this is even truer for preschoolers. To get the most out of your Disney World visit with the kids, think of the trip in terms of total experience and not just a vacation that revolves around riding attractions.

Preschoolers love colors, music, motion, and surprise; Disney has all these and then some. Afternoon parades are a whirl of color, sound, and movement. Nightly fireworks shows will amaze and astound you with their elaborate choreography to music. Meeting a favorite character will make a story or movie come to life. Delight in seeing something unexpected. Be transported to another time and place through the theming of the parks and resorts. Transform your family vacation into one filled with wonderment and amazement. Experience the magic.

Should You Go?

There is nothing in the proverbial parent manual that says you have to take your kids to Disney World, or that your preschoolers must meet Mickey Mouse by age five or else their emotional development will be stunted. Sharing a Disney World vacation with your kids can be a magical, memorable experience, but some kids are not ready for it as early as others. After all, why spend the time and money for a Disney World vacation if your children aren't ready to enjoy it? On the other hand, many families with older children also have a preschooler in tow and would like to make the Walt Disney World trip memorable for the entire family, little ones included.

Is Your Child Ready for a Disney World Vacation?

Every child has a unique personality and temperament. As a parent, you are best equipped to decide if and when you should take your child to Disney World. Here are some important considerations.

Attention Span. Many of the best Disney attractions are not rides at all; they are either live stage shows or theater attractions. If your child is very active or unused to watching television at home, it may be a chore to focus and sit still for a 20-30 minute show. Does your small child have the attention span and capability to sit quietly during these types of attractions?

Standing for an Extended Period of Time. A Disney World vacation will involve waiting in lines for attractions; strollers are not permitted in attraction queues. FASTPASS can be used to minimize wait time but it is unlikely to eliminate it entirely. Another factor to consider is the preshow. Some Disney preshow areas do not offer benches and are standing room only. Are your toddlers or preschoolers able to stand by themselves for extended periods of time? Is there someone in your traveling party who is willing to hold them if they cannot?

Waiting…Waiting…Waiting. "How much longer?" is the Disney World equivalent to "Are we there yet?" Will your kids be able to wait patiently without having a meltdown or causing you to have one? Luckily, the Disney queues are extremely well themed and have lots of opportunities for your kids to pass the time enjoyably. See Chapter 4, "Touring," for ideas on entertaining kids while in line.

Dining. If your family is planning a number of table-service meals, consider whether the kids will sit still while waiting for their meals to arrive. Do your children eat more quickly than the adults in your party and will they patiently play with crayons and other small, quiet toys while the rest of the family finishes dinner? Have you considered buffets, character dining, or dinner shows to help your children enjoy mealtimes?

 If your toddlers use sippy cups and toddler utensils, **TIP** don't forget to pack them in your theme park bag.

Fear Factors. Many of the Disney World attractions, which may not be considered particularly scary, have either a darkened preshow area, theater, or ride track. Volume may also be a factor. Many shows have loud music or sounds. Is your child uncomfortable in the dark or with loud noises?

Sleep Schedules. How many naps do your toddlers and preschoolers take? When and how long do they nap? Will your children have a meltdown if they miss a nap? Are you willing to miss the nightly entertainment if the kids need to turn in early?

Costumed Characters. Disney World has many Character Greeting areas. Is your child afraid of large costumed characters? Kids may be more comfortable meeting "face" characters such as Snow White or Aladdin who do not wear masks, instead of costumed characters like Mickey Mouse. If your child does not enjoy the Character Greetings, it is fairly easy to avoid them.

Budget. The cost of a Walt Disney World vacation can add up quickly; this is especially true with larger travel parties. You'll have to purchase theme park tickets, lodging, food, and those inevitable souvenirs. If a Disney World vacation is going to be a once-in-a-childhood experience for your child, waiting a few more years is probably best. Older children will be able to experience more attractions and remember the trip long into adulthood. Parents won't be restricted by sleep schedules, tired feet, and shorter attention spans.

Planning the Trip

To Travel Agent or Not to Travel Agent

A perennial question is whether to use a travel agent or not. Travel agents specializing in Disney vacations will often have access to discounts before they are available to the general public and can continue to apply discounts to your vacation as they are released by Disney. Sometimes it is no small feat to manage all the details of putting together a Walt Disney World trip to include dining and recreation bookings – a reputable travel agent adds a lot of value by doing so.

If you decide to use an agent, you'll want to look for an agent who doesn't charge agency fees, even for changes and cancellations (Disney may pass on change fees to you); the agent's commission will be paid by Disney. It is important to select an Authorized Disney Vacation Planner who has graduated from the Disney College of Knowledge to ensure familiarity with all Walt Disney World has to offer. For my money, I would prefer an agent who not only is trained to book Disney vacations, but who has traveled to the Walt Disney World Resort recently. A travel agent who has been a Walt Disney World guest is more likely to be able to answer your "real-world" questions and offer practical advice – there is no substitute for experiencing the resort.

Finding a Disney travel specialist is no different from finding any other service provider – ask around and do your research. The Disney community is a great resource. Visit message boards and the large Disney-related websites for recommendations.

Time of Year to Visit

There are two major benefits to visiting Walt Disney World when schools are in session; you can save a great deal of money and the crowds are much lighter. Keep in mind some areas of the country resume classes in early August. Like many vacation destinations, Walt Disney World defines vacation seasons and the lodging rates are adjusted accordingly. The most expensive times to visit are generally those weeks that correspond with school vacations, including the summer months. For lower crowd levels, also avoid the weeks that flank the school holiday weeks, and the summer months. The difference can be waiting 15 minutes to ride the popular attractions versus a 90-minute wait.

Summer and winter vacations can be less than ideal for families with preschoolers. The summer months can be extremely hot and humid in Florida, which can make for a difficult trip with red-faced, whining children. On the flip side, the winter months in the Orlando area can be quite chilly at times, particularly in the evenings. Considering that you'll be outdoors much of the time, traveling with young children during this time of the year can be hit or miss – not something you want when planning a magical trip. I recommend planning your Walt Disney World vacation during the spring and fall months. October and early November are my absolute favorite times of the year to visit. The weather is mild and the crowds are relatively light.

 Research special events that are planned during the time you want to visit; you may rethink your week. For example, events, such as cheer competitions, that involve large groups may mean the Value Resorts are more crowded and filled with team spirit and the noise that goes along with it.

Events that may increase crowds include Disney Marathon weekends, school breaks for international tour groups, Star Wars weekends, Gay Days, Epcot Food and Wine Festival, "Jersey Week," Pop Warner Super Bowl, and National Cheer and Dance Championship.

 Walt Disney World uses Holiday or Seasonal Pricing on dining. The price of meals at some restaurants will increase during high-demand times of the year. Similarly, Disney dining plans are priced according to season.

 For the past few years, Walt Disney World has offered free dining with vacations booked during late

August/September. There is no guarantee this promotion will be offered every year but it is something to keep in mind when planning the time of year you will visit.

Room-Only Reservations versus Packages

With room-only rates, you'll reserve lodging only. You will then need to purchase tickets and other recreational activities a la carte. Walt Disney World offers different Magic Your Way packages, which include lodging and tickets. The biggest advantage to these packages is the Disney Dining Plans. Disney Dining Plans allow you to pre-pay for your food and are available only to guests who book a Magic Your Way package (lodging plus tickets), Annual Passholders, or Disney Vacation Club members.

Some additional advantages to the Magic Your Way packages are ease of booking and the possibility of saving money – many of the promotions are package deals. When making your decision, consider that packages may offer extras, some of which you may not use. Also, packages must be paid for in their entirety prior to the vacation.

Whether a room-only reservation has better cancellation terms than a package depends on when you cancel and the category of lodging you reserved. With a room-only reservation, if you cancel within five days of travel (six for reservations made online), you forfeit your one night's deposit, plus tax. If you're staying in a Deluxe Resort, this can be costly. With a package, if you cancel within 45 days, you are subject to a $200 charge.

Carefully review the different packages against a room-only reservation. Compare costs including the Disney Dining Plan versus out-of-pocket dining and planned recreational activities.

Weeknight (Sunday through Thursday) rates are less than weekend (Friday and Saturday) nights for most resorts.

Tickets

Another decision you'll have to make is the type of tickets to purchase. The base ticket allows you to visit one theme park per day. The more days you purchase, the lower the daily cost of admission. For example, an adult, one-day, base Disney World theme park ticket is $85; a seven-day ticket is about $38 per day. You can purchase a Park Hopper Option for $55 that allows you to visit different theme parks within the same day. This is convenient if you make dining reservations for a restaurant in a different theme park, or park hop to attend a parade or nightly entertainment. Options to visit water parks, DisneyQuest®, Disney's Wide World of Sports®, and golfing are available for an additional cost. You may also add a No Expiration Option. Tickets expire 14 days after first use; with the No Expiration Option, the tickets never expire. Compute your break-even point before adding this option; the savings may be negligible. Adding the No Expiration Option to an adult ticket is an extra $12.50 per day for a two-day ticket and $22.85 per day for a seven-day ticket.

 For families with preschoolers, you'll most likely visit only a single park per day so the base ticket should be fine if you do some advance planning. Unsure? You can upgrade your ticket during your visit if necessary.

 Children under the age of three do not require a park ticket. Also, kids under three eat free at family style and buffet restaurants. Many buffet restaurants offer character dining, and are a great opportunity for your toddlers to meet their favorite Disney friends free of charge.

 TIP Disney World theme park tickets are pricey. For your protection, make a photocopy of the back of your pre-purchased park tickets prior to leaving home. If you purchase your paper tickets at Walt Disney World, a cell phone picture will work just as well. In the unfortunate event you lose your tickets, the photocopy or digital picture with the ticket's identifying information will help Guest Services correct the situation quickly.

 TIP Undercover Tourist (www.undercovertourist.com) is a highly recommended Internet seller of discount Disney tickets. The best part: they are a Disney Selected Ticket Seller so you can be sure you will receive unused tickets and not vouchers or other gimmicks. Discounts are about 10 percent and free shipping is offered. When comparing prices, remember that Undercover Tourist includes tax in quoted ticket prices while Disney does not. For even more savings, sign up for the MouseSavers (www.mousesavers.com) newsletter for an exclusive Undercover Tourist discount.

Getting Ready for Your Disney Trip

Preparing Your Child

By both subtly and not so subtly preparing your child for a Disney vacation, you'll increase the enchantment of the trip.

Introduction to Characters. To a young child, the larger-than-life costumed characters can be frightening and overwhelming. There are many Character Greetings throughout Walt Disney

World, and it is best to know beforehand if your child will excitedly look forward to the character meet and greets or run terrified in the other direction.

If your toddlers are scared of Santa Claus or the Easter Bunny, this will provide some indication of how they might react to the Disney characters. Look for opportunities to interact with costumed characters prior to the trip. Many local stores have promotional events featuring mascots or characters. Local amusement parks often have costumed characters as well.

Oftentimes children are unprepared for the sheer size of a character; they don't equate Tigger on a page in a book as being the same height as Daddy in real life. Before the trip, you can explain that Tigger will be as tall as Daddy or show them some pictures of Tigger next to a small child.

Sleeping Away from Home. Walt Disney World can be both exciting and overwhelming for little ones. Couple this with the fact that your children will not be in their own beds and there may be some anxiety. Hotel rooms have their own unique sounds, temperatures, and layouts. If you have the opportunity to plan a couple of small overnight trips prior to your Disney vacation, take advantage of it to help your child become comfortable sleeping in different rooms and beds.

 Packing a small nightlight or leaving the bathroom light on and the door slightly ajar can help ease nighttime anxieties. Try to keep the bedtime routine as familiar as possible; read a favorite story and don't forget any comfort items your child sleeps with.

TIP Temperatures in a hotel can be difficult to control. Bringing different weight pajamas can help your kids feel comfortable even with temperatures warmer or cooler than at home.

Familiarity with Disney Characters. Disney has so many sights and sounds to delight the senses that familiarity with the Disney characters and storylines is not necessary. However, some previous exposure will enhance your preschooler's experience. Depending on your child's age and interests, reading Disney storybooks, watching Disney DVDs, visiting Disney Junior online, or playing with Disney toys will help introduce your small child to the Disney family of characters and stories.

Travel Agent in Training. Enlist your child's help to plan the trip. Order a free Walt Disney World planning DVD at www.disneyworld.com and watch it as a family. Visit the Disney World website and look at the color photos of the resorts and attractions. Create a customized map together and have it shipped to your house. Visit a video sharing site and watch clips of Disney stage shows, attractions, and parades; preview content first to avoid "stranger danger." Watch your child's reactions during planning to get a sense of any attractions that may make your child uncomfortable and the ones that are a "must-do."

Anticipation

One of the most exciting parts of any vacation is the anticipation. Try these ideas to pump up your kids for their Disney World trip.

Trip Countdown. Create a simple tear-away countdown calendar to build anticipation for an upcoming Disney vacation. The countdown calendar can be decorated with Disney stickers, stamps, and hole-punches.

Welcome Letter and Invitations. What better way to get your kids excited about a Disney World trip than for them to receive a welcome letter from Mickey Mouse or their favorite Disney character? They would also be thrilled to receive a personalized invitation to whatever character dining or special events your family has planned. Custom T-shirts with a graphic of their favorite character, or Cinderella Castle, and a personalized message will make them feel like princes or princesses.

Autograph Book. Get creative and design and create a custom autograph book with your kids. You can design a single Disney-inspired autograph sheet or even custom sheets for particular characters. See Chapter 8, "Recreation," for more information on character meets and greets and autograph books.

Packing

Clothing. Temperatures can fluctuate significantly from early morning to midday to evening in Florida. If you are going to be away from the hotel room for an extended period of time, dress your family in layers or bring a lightweight sweater or jacket for the spring/summer evening hours. Heavier outerwear during fall/winter days and evenings is often necessary.

 Pack each of your child's outfits, including undergarments and socks, in a zip lock bag. Dressing in the morning will be smoother since each outfit is already coordinated and complete. Simply hand your child or another adult the zip lock bag when it is time to get ready for the day. Save the zip lock bags for wet bathing suits, snacks for the parks, or to protect valuables on water rides. Always supervise small children with plastic zip lock bags.

Afternoon showers are a given during the summer months. Purchasing rain ponchos at Disney World is expensive (adult $8.50; child $7.50); look for inexpensive ones at your local big box store, such as Walmart.

Diapers. Diapers are available throughout Disney World but they are costly and only the most common sizes are available – bring your own. Since diapers are bulky, consider shipping them to your resort in advance or having them delivered by a local grocery store. When packages are properly addressed, your resort bell stand will be happy to hold them until your arrival. Contact your Disney World resort for more specifics.

 Short on time? JetSetBabies (www.jetsetbabies.com) **TIP** and Babies Travel Lite (www.babiestravellite.com) will package and ship baby and toddler supplies to your hotel.

Medical. It is difficult for a parent to watch a child suffer from an injury or illness. It is more unfortunate when it occurs far away from home. As a precautionary measure, ensure you have a copy of your insurance card; the name, address, and phone number of your child's pediatrician; a list of any allergies; and a list of medications your child takes.

Security Check. Disney parks have security checks prior to entering. Guests must open up all compartments of bags. Bring a theme park bag with as few pockets as possible to make your park entry just a little smoother.

Living the Magic

Magical Gifts. Fun, inexpensive Disney-related items can be purchased prior to your Disney trip. Watch your child's eyes light up to find a small, special present left by a favorite Disney character in the room. Examples are sunglasses, Disney coloring books, autograph books, pens, and stickers.

Disney's Enchanted Call. For only $2.50, schedule a special phone call from one of eleven beloved Disney characters or princesses. Visit https://secure.uvoxnetworks.com/disney.

The Multi-generational Trip

Vacationing at Walt Disney World with family is all about aligning expectations. Bottom line: Do your expectations match those of your traveling companions? Seems simple, doesn't it? The answer, of course, is a magical vacation. But if you want to return from the trip still on speaking terms and with your relationships intact, there's more, a whole lot more, to discuss before you start making your reservations.

The Child Care Talk

One of the most common Walt Disney World travel groups is families with grandparents. Traveling with grandparents is a wonderful experience for everyone, but Grandma and Grandpa may have different expectations for the trip than Mom and Dad. Extended family may feel as if they are expected to be glorified babysitters and it's important to reassure them that is not the case; it's their vacation too. If you would like an adult night or two out, discuss it with your family and ask if family members are comfortable watching the kids. If they aren't, make a reservation at the Children's Activity Centers or Kid's Nite Out so everyone enjoys their time at Walt Disney World.

Togetherness

Just how much togetherness is right for your extended family?

Lodging. Is bunking together in a DVC vacation home or a family suite the right choice? It may be, especially if you're traveling with Grandma and Grandpa. On the other hand if your little one is up at 5 a.m. and Grandpa can't function before 9 a.m., you may want to rethink the whole staying together thing.

What happens when one part of the group expects to stay at a Deluxe Resort while a Value is in the budget for the other half of the group? If two or more rooms are the way to go for your group, talk about preferences for budget and theming early on. Logistically, it's more convenient to stay at the same resort. It's easier to meet at the resort bus stop than to have to coordinate another meeting place and depend on Disney transportation to get you to the right place at the right time.

Alone Time. Talk about how much time you'll spend together at Walt Disney World. For some families, it's best to split up throughout the day and then get back together for dinner while others wouldn't dream of touring the Magic Kingdom without the whole group.

Chef Mickey or Chefs de France? If you're not careful, meals could turn into a showdown between grandparents who prefer signature dining and the kids who want nothing more than to dine with the Fab Five.

Consider what is the right mix of group meals versus going it alone. When we travel with my extended family, we eat about 75 percent of our table-service meals together. Other families wouldn't consider anything but eating together every meal.

Expenses

Disney World is one of those places where you can either spend a little (relatively speaking) or a lot. You'll have great experiences either way – they'll just be different. Here are some things to discuss with your group before you leave home.

Who Pays? Where money is involved, discussing expectations is paramount. Are you inviting your parents as your guests and do you plan on picking up the tab for everything besides personal expenses? Or, will you be vacationing together but everyone is responsible for their own costs? If you share lodging, how will the room be paid for? When your group eats at table-service restaurants, will you rotate who picks up the bill or will you have the server bring two checks? Don't forget incidentals the whole group will share such as water and snacks delivered from a service such as Garden Grocer. It's uncomfortable to talk money but defining expectations in a sensitive way early in the planning process will avoid any awkward misunderstandings later.

Extras. Walt Disney World has recreation, special tours, and more for every budget. Problem is, not every budget may have room for these extras. One approach is to tour the theme parks together and then take a midday break where people can go their separate ways – it may be a nap and pool time for some or golf for others. Before booking any additional activities, be sure to be upfront about the additional costs with your family.

Touring

Commando, Leisurely, or Somewhere in the Middle.
Deciding on a general touring plan before you visit the park is essential. Active grandparents may not be used to taking a break

midday so that preschoolers can rest. Discuss your child's general schedule with your family and decide if the whole group will take a nap in the room or if some adults will hit the thrill rides or get in a little shopping while the kids rest.

After you agree on a general touring style, you have to talk about a daily schedule. Does your group plan on taking advantage of Extra Magic Hours? Do you plan on visiting more than one park each day and does everyone in your group agree to the extra cost of a Park Hopper Option on their ticket?

Dumbo the Flying Elephant or Rock 'n' Roller Coaster.
Small kids generally tend to dictate the attraction selection. For a successful group trip, pick rides that interest everyone when you tour as a group. Save the thrill rides for when you split up or take advantage of Rider Swap.

Other Advance Planning Tips

Walt Disney World Moms Panel. Have a question about your trip? Submit a question or search the archives at the Walt Disney World Moms Panel (www.disneyworldmoms.com).

Put on Your Walking Shoes. Prepare for the miles of walking you'll be doing at the parks and bond with your family at the same time by "training" for Disney World with daily walks.

Groceries. Depending on your accommodations, consider purchasing groceries to prepare simple meals. There are local delivery services that will deliver groceries to your Walt Disney World resort (see "Resources"). The bell stands will refrigerate perishable groceries until your arrival. Additionally, you can ship non-perishables to your resort. Contact your resort for specifics.

Refrigerators are available at all Walt Disney World resorts. They are free of charge in the Deluxe and Moderate Resorts. Rentals are about $10 per day at the Value Resorts. Resort food courts and snack areas have a microwave and toaster for guest use. This is handy if you bring instant oatmeal packets or the like from home.

Beverages. Staying hydrated is a must in the warm Florida weather. However, purchasing bottled water or other beverages at Walt Disney World is expensive.

 Consider purchasing a refillable mug, available at Walt Disney World resorts. Once the mugs are purchased, you may fill them, free of charge, at the beverage station in your Disney resort's food court or quick-service location. You may not refill them at the parks. The beverage stations contain sodas, fruit drinks, coffee, tea, and hot chocolate, but not milk or juice. The free refills are only good for the duration of your trip (not for future trips). A refillable mug is about $15; it pays for itself after six uses.

 If you are driving to Walt Disney World or are renting a car at the airport, make a brief stop at an off-site store to purchase water. Also, local grocery services such as Garden Grocer (www.gardengrocer.com) and WeGoShop (www.wegoshop.com) or national companies like Staples will deliver water to your hotel. Even with the delivery charge, chances are you will save money over purchasing bottled water in the parks. Disney recycles water bottles.

 A green option is to refill a reusable water bottle with tap water. Add flavored mixes if you don't care for the taste of tap water.

Quick-service, or counter-service, locations will provide a cup of ice water at no charge.

Souvenirs. Souvenir purchases can be a source of tension. Put a plan in place prior to the trip. For example, you may decide to give your kids a small amount of money to spend as they wish – no questions asked. You might allow your child to select one item per day as long as it is less than X dollars.

 Stop at Guest Relations in the Disney theme parks or at your Disney resort's concierge to purchase Disney Dollars for your kids to use for souvenir purchases.

 Have your kids earn credits toward Disney Dollars by doing extra chores at home.

 Disney's Rewards® Visa® Card. The Chase Disney Rewards Visa credit or debit card rewards you with Disney Dollars. Consider using the Disney Rewards card to purchase souvenirs and meals.

Pets. A kennel operated by Best Friends Pet Care, Inc. is available on Walt Disney World property. Kennels provide daily or overnight boarding for pets. Resort reservations do not guarantee your pet a space in the kennel; reservations are suggested. Refer to "Resources" for the phone number.

2   Disney Lodging

On-Site Benefits

There are many different options for lodging at Walt Disney World – both on-site and off-site. These options fulfill any family's preferences for budget, location, theming, and amenities. Staying on-site can be more expensive but offers additional benefits that make vacationing with the preschool set easier. *The Unofficial Guide to Walt Disney World* by Bob Sehlinger, Menasha Ridge, and Len Testa is an excellent resource for off-site accommodations.

Disney's Magical Express. Complimentary, round-trip bus transportation from the Orlando International Airport to the Walt Disney World Resort is offered to guests staying on-site. When using the Magical Express, bypass the luggage claim; your bags will be delivered to your hotel room within a few hours. Refer to Chapter 3, "Transportation," for more information.

Free Transportation around the "World." As a Walt Disney World guest, you'll enjoy free transportation around Disney World. This includes bus, monorail, and boat transportation.

When your child needs a break from it all, it is a relief to know that you can board complimentary transportation, sit back, and relax for the return trip to your resort.

As an added benefit, you won't have to rent and install a car seat in a rental car. This task is difficult and can be downright frustrating in an unfamiliar car.

 TIP It takes less time to get to certain theme parks from some resorts than others. If you plan on spending most of your time at one park, factor transportation travel time into your lodging decision.

Extra Magic Hours. Every day, one of the theme parks opens an hour earlier or stays open up to three hours later for Walt Disney World resort guests. Being at the park when it first opens, for the Extra Magic Hour, helps you beat the heat, crowds, and lines while giving you the opportunity to return to the resort for a break in the afternoon before heading out for an evening of dining and fun.

Package Delivery. Inevitably, you will be purchasing souvenirs for your small kids. There is limited space to store packages in strollers. As a security precaution, you also won't want to leave the packages in your unattended stroller. Walt Disney World will deliver purchased packages to the resort where you are staying.

Your "Key to the World." As a Walt Disney World resort guest your room key also provides charging privileges, which allows you to reduce the amount of cash you carry. You will be charged at check-out. Admittedly, this benefit can also have disadvantages as it is easier to lose track of your spending.

Advance Dining Reservation (ADR) Advantage. ADRs can be booked 180 days in advance. Many of you reading this are thinking, "What! I have to plan my dining six months out?" That's exactly what you need to do to secure reservations at your preferred time at the most popular restaurants and dining experiences during the busiest weeks of the year or when a Free Dining promotion is offered. Guests staying on-site can begin booking their ADRs 180 prior to their arrival date and make reservations for the entire vacation, up to 10 days. This is effectively a 180 + 10 day booking window. This slight advantage may help you get that elusive dining reservation at Cinderella's Royal Table or Chef Mickey's.

Toddler Sleeping Accommodations. All Disney resorts have Pack N Play cribs and sheets available, but a blanket is not provided; the rooms can get chilly so remember to pack one. Resorts also have removable bed rails for older children. Reserve them when you make your reservation to be sure they will be available for your stay.

 TIP If you have a child who is too big to sleep comfortably in a Pack N Play but is not comfortable sleeping in a bed, try a child-sized air mattress. These mattresses are comfortable, fold easily for travel, and usually contain an electric air pump. I bought ours from One Step Ahead (www.onestepahead.com).

Online Check-in. The Walt Disney World Resort offers online check-in to facilitate the arrival process. Guests may check in online 10 days prior to their check-in date. Once you arrive at the resort, stop at the online check-in desk, present photo ID, and pick up your envelope with everything you need.

Mobile Room Ready Notification Service. Arriving early? Take advantage of Disney's Mobile Room Ready Notification Service by providing a cell phone number upon check-in. When your room is ready, you'll receive either an automated call or a text message, depending on your preference. Leave your luggage at the bell stand and enjoy the parks or a leisurely lunch.

Free Parking at Disney Parks. With your Disney resort ID, enjoy complimentary parking at the theme parks.

 Special Occasions. If your child is celebrating a special occasion during your Walt Disney World visit, mention it at the Front Desk while checking in and when making dining reservations. Buttons are available for most celebratory occasions. When Cast Members see the button, they will often make your child feel special by mentioning the event or by doing something out of the ordinary for your child, such as providing a FASTPASS for a popular attraction, or offering a free dessert.

Special-occasion cakes can be ordered using The Cake Hotline at 407-827-2253. Please order your cake at least 48 hours in advance.

 If you are an eligible guest (i.e., an active or retired member of the military or a Department of Defense civilian), consider staying at the beautiful Shades of Green Resort on Walt Disney World property. It is not a Walt Disney World resort, as it is owned by and operated as an Armed Forces Recreation Center. Therefore, many of the on-site perks do not apply. For example, the Walt Disney World buses do not stop at Shades of Green; however, Shades of Green provides its own buses. By staying at this resort, which has some of the largest rooms on the property, you can save a tremendous amount of money on your lodging when compared with similar Disney resorts.

Shades of Green also sells discounted Disney theme park tickets for eligible Walt Disney World guests. Note that you do not have to stay at the resort to purchase these tickets.

Visit www.shadesofgreen.org for eligibility requirements.

Choosing a Disney World Resort Category

Disney resorts are categorized as Deluxe Resorts, Moderate Resorts, and Value Resorts. Additionally, there is a campsite at Disney's Fort Wilderness Resort. The most obvious differences among the three resort categories are price points. Deluxe Resorts are more costly while Value Resorts are the most budget-friendly.

Families should consider the features of each resort category, in addition to the nightly room rate, when selecting a Disney World resort category. Generally, rooms sleep four guests comfortably, not including a child under three who sleeps in a Pack N Play. Additional charges apply for more than two adults in the room. Always confirm the room rate for your party size with your reservation agent prior to booking your reservation.

Deluxe Resorts

Deluxe Resorts provide the greatest number of amenities, offer rooms that are bit larger, tend to be quieter, and have the most convenient locations. Disney transportation is more varied; guests often have their choice of monorail, bus, or boat transportation. In my opinion, Disney pays more attention to landscaping and pool theming at the Deluxe Resorts.

The nightly room rate will vary based on the Deluxe Resort, the season, and the type of room. For a standard room, rates range

from $265 per night in Value Season to $730 per night in
Holiday Season.

The Deluxe Resorts are Animal Kingdom Lodge, Contemporary
Resort, Beach Club Resort, Boardwalk Inn, Grand Floridian
Resort & Spa, Polynesian Resort, Walt Disney World Swan and
Dolphin Resort, Wilderness Lodge, and Yacht Club Resort.

Location. The "monorail resorts," categorized as Deluxe
Resorts, are those that are accessible from the Magic Kingdom
monorail loop. Guests may board the monorail that stops at the
Magic Kingdom directly from their resort. Families of young
children who spend most of their time at the Magic Kingdom
theme park will enjoy this convenience. The Boardwalk area
resorts, within walking distance of Epcot and Disney's
Hollywood Studios, are also classified as Deluxe Resorts.

Amenities. Many of the finer resort restaurants are located at
Disney's Deluxe Resorts. These locations offer a snack shop for
quick-service items but do not offer a large food court with a
more varied selection.

If your family is interested in shopping, the Deluxe Resorts have
higher-end stores.

Most of the Deluxe Resorts are located on the water and provide
recreational activities, boat rentals, and a bit of a sandy beach.

The Children's Activity Centers, which provide child care during
the evenings, are located at the Deluxe Resorts. Although you do
not have to be a guest at the resort to make a reservation, it is
convenient to have them located at the same resort as your room.

Animal Kingdom Lodge. This expansive resort received the AAA Four-Diamond award in 2011. Its accolades are well-deserved. The beautifully designed African-inspired resort is home to exotic animals who roam the savannah. Imagine your little one's excitement waking up and seeing giraffe, zebra, and wildebeest outside the windows of select rooms or from one of the resort's viewing areas. The pools and restaurants are top-notch. So, what don't I like about this resort? I am disappointed that you cannot walk to the Animal Kingdom theme park but must take a Disney bus or your own transportation. Also, for the safety of the animals, balloons are not allowed in the resort.

Beach Club Resort. The Boardwalk area is one of my favorites; guests can walk through the International Gateway to Epcot or take a longer, 15-minute walk to Disney Hollywood Studios.

And that's not all. The Boardwalk has convenient access to entertainment, dining, and a great boardwalk to stroll or pedal around on a surrey bike. This small resort is the closest to Epcot's International Gateway and captures the relaxed nature of beach living with a very welcoming atmosphere. Perhaps the best feature is the Stormalong Bay pool area. Pool area is a bit of a misnomer; this incredible water park has a natural sand-bottom pool, waterfalls, a huge waterslide, and a slow-moving river.

Boardwalk Inn. As the name suggests, this resort is part of the Disney Boardwalk area and is inspired by Atlantic City during the early to mid-part of the 20th century. The Inn is beautiful with an element of fun and whimsy that extends to the old wooden roller coaster-themed feature pool. Lounge chairs and seating arrangements on the balcony off the Inn's lobby practically beckon one to sink down, relax, and enjoy some people-watching. Located on the Boardwalk, the Inn boasts the same closeness to Epcot and Disney's Hollywood Studios as the other Boardwalk area resorts. Strolling on the Boardwalk in the evening and taking in the nightly entertainment is a great way to end a busy day in the theme parks. One negative is that there is no on-site dining. Even though there are a number of eateries on the Boardwalk that are easily accessed by guests of the Boardwalk Inn, they aren't all the most kid-friendly.

Contemporary Resort. Located on the Magic Kingdom monorail loop, there's a lot to like about this Disney resort. The proximity to the Magic Kingdom is a huge plus for young families. Add in the fact that the monorail runs directly through the center of the resort and the coolness factor has been ramped up. Make a reservation at the California Grill and you'll enjoy stunning vistas and an incredible view of Wishes, Magic Kingdom's nighttime fireworks spectacular. I also love that it is only a short walk from the resort to the Magic Kingdom. The updated décor is beautiful with its contemporary feel and understated neutral color palette. Downside? The grounds are not as extensive as those at other resorts and the main pool is a bit ho-hum for me.

Grand Floridian Resort & Spa. This elegant resort is breathtaking and has a rich and luxurious feel to it. The attentive service is undeniable. Soothing sounds greet you as a piano player tickles the ivories in the lobby. The marble floor is inlaid with images of classic Disney characters. High-end amenities include 5-star dining, upscale shops, and a spa (currently undergoing a refurbishment). The Grand Floridian is located on the Magic Kingdom monorail loop so getting to the Magic Kingdom is a breeze. There is a zero-entry pool, a beach to lounge on, and watercraft rentals. Depending on your taste, this resort may feel a bit formal compared with other Disney lodging choices. Also, keep in mind that most of the restaurants are not as relaxed and preschooler-friendly as at other resorts.

Polynesian Resort. Lush, topical foliage. Volcano rising above the zero-entry pool. Leis when you check-in. Cast Members greeting you with a friendly "Aloha." A mini tropical "rainforest" in the lobby. Torches illuminating the walkways on a dark night. These are some of the reasons the Polynesian Resort is one of my favorites – the laid-back atmosphere is right up my alley. To me, the location is ideal. Not only can you easily use the monorail to get to the Magic Kingdom, but a short, scenic walk to the Transportation and Ticket Center provides direct access to the Epcot monorail. The beach is the perfect spot to watch Wishes or the Electrical Water Pageant. One drawback for foodies is the lack of Signature Dining restaurants. Also, although the rooms are large, attractive, and comfortable, some guests may feel the relaxed theming is not sufficiently upscale for a Deluxe Resort.

Walt Disney World Swan and Dolphin Resort. This is not a Walt Disney World resort even though it is located in the Walt Disney World Boardwalk resort area. These large hotels, popular with convention crowds, are centrally located and house restaurants that have received many accolades. A clear benefit is the year-round deals offered. They also enjoy the same benefits as other hotels in the Boardwalk resort area such as nightly entertainment and proximity to two of the four theme parks. Two of the biggest negatives are that Swan and Dolphin guests are not eligible for Disney dining plans and Disney's Magical Express. Another negative is that guests must pay an additional daily rate to park a car. Lastly, the hotels do not provide as immersive an experience as the Disney resorts but do have a lap pool and a large, freeform main pool.

TIP The Walt Disney World Swan and Dolphin Resort frequently offers special rates and packages for the military (active and retired), nurses, teachers, and school support staff.

Wilderness Lodge. The large Pacific Northwest log-cabin aesthetic of this resort is breathtaking. The design reflects the style of national park lodges at the beginning of the 20th century and the exterior resembles a tricked-out Lincoln Log cabin. Don't let the phrase "log cabin" fool you, this lodge is well-appointed and there's nothing rustic about it. Amazing features abound, from the huge fireplace to the creek that meanders from the lobby outside to the swimming pool with its waterfall, to the "geyser," which erupts every hour; it's a child's paradise. It's also home to a couple of popular restaurants. This resort is particularly spectacular at Christmastime. Unfortunately, this resort is not part of the Magic Kingdom monorail loop.

Yacht Club Resort. The stately nautical theme is in full force at this classy New England-style hotel. The dark blues and burnished wood tones throughout the resort are gorgeous and relaxing. To me, this resort is a bit quieter and slightly more formal than the neighboring Beach Club Resort. The Yacht Club Resort adjoins the Beach Club Resort so they share the magnificent Stormalong Bay pool area. A stay at this resort includes all the benefits and amenities of the Boardwalk area resorts: primarily entertainment, dining, and proximity to Epcot and Disney's Hollywood Studios. A favorite pastime for my family is a frozen treat at the nearby Beaches & Cream Soda Shop. Depending on your viewpoint, a downside of the Beach & Yacht Club Resort, the Boardwalk Inn, and the Swan and Dolphin Resort is that there is no bus service to Epcot or

Hollywood Studios. Guests either walk or take one of the
Friendship boats.

Moderate Resorts

The grounds at the Moderate Resorts are beautiful, spacious, and
perfect for a family stroll. Disney transportation to the theme
parks, with the exception of the Cabins at Fort Wilderness, is
limited to buses. These large resorts have multiple bus stops
within the resort itself, which can increase transportation time to
the theme parks. The rooms at these resorts are generally located
in moderately-sized guest buildings situated throughout the
grounds. Double beds are standard at most of the moderate
resorts. The most significant difference between the different
Moderate Resorts is theming. Prior to your stay, review the
resort map. Request a room near the bus transportation stop, or
seriously consider bringing your own stroller for the walk back
to your room. After a tiring day at the theme parks, a long walk
to your room with exhausted children can seem like an eternity.

For a standard room, rates range from $159 in Value Season to
$455 per night during Holiday Season.

The Moderate Resorts are the Cabins at Fort Wilderness Resort,
Caribbean Beach Resort, Coronado Springs Resort, Port Orleans
French Quarter, and Port Orleans Riverside.

Amenities. In addition to a restaurant, most Moderate Resorts
offer an extensive food court with a wide variety of foods and
enough seating to accommodate large numbers of guests. This is
convenient when dining with toddlers and preschoolers.

With their larger spaces, Moderate Resorts commonly offer bicycle or surrey bike rentals and other recreational activities for kids. They also have several options for watercraft rentals.

Cabins at Fort Wilderness Resort. There's a lot to like about the Cabins at Fort Wilderness Resort, especially the plentiful recreation options including the two pool areas. Each cabin sleeps six and has a small kitchen and a separate bedroom, unlike standard Disney resort rooms. Best of all, kids can be kids without disturbing other guests. The cabins also have outdoor grill sites and guests enjoy some of the most unspoiled Florida landscape at the Walt Disney World Resort. Nature lovers will have lots of quiet trails to roam and will likely spot friendly wildlife such as ducks and geese. However, during the summer months, insects may be an issue. Once you enter Fort Wilderness Resort, cars are parked and may not travel within the resort areas. However, an internal bus and rental golf carts (reserve ahead) are available to make it easier to access the dining, shopping, and recreation available at the resort. The somewhat remote location means dining options outside the resort are not easily accessible; dining within the resort is limited.

Caribbean Beach Resort. This resort celebrates the spirit of Caribbean island life. The widespread resort is full of colorful guest buildings, grouped into five areas. The feature pool, modeled after a fort with pirate cannons, is spectacular and makes me wish I were a kid again. The reception area, with check-in and guest services, may be quite a distance from your room. The same is true of the feature pool and dining options. Disney recognizes this and there are multiple bus stops throughout the resort area that provide access to the theme parks or other areas of the Caribbean Beach Resort; multiple stops within the resort may add a few minutes to your theme park "commute." The resort restaurants are the only easily accessible dining options – you cannot walk or quickly hop on a monorail to other dining options.

 TIP Your little pirates will enjoy the themed pirate rooms at Disney's Caribbean Beach Resort. These specially decorated rooms contain pirate beds and other custom details to immerse your family in the pirate experience. You will pay about a $25 premium per night to stay in these rooms.

Coronado Springs Resort. Spanish explorer Francisco Vasquez de Coronado, and his quest for gold, partly inspired the Coronado Springs Resort's theming. This lovely southwestern-styled resort, with its gorgeous lobby, encircles a large lake. Lago Dorado is the perfect backdrop for a jog or bike ride. Don't miss the Mayan-themed feature pool with its large pyramid or the imaginative children's playground. Relax with your family by renting some pedal boats. Like most of the sprawling Moderate Resorts, Coronado Springs has multiple bus stops throughout the resort. This is especially convenient for reaching the food and recreation amenities that may be quite a distance from your room. Coronado Springs stands apart its peers in that standard rooms offer queen-size instead of double beds. There is also a health club on the premises, an amenity typically reserved for the Deluxe Resorts.

There are no other Disney resorts in close proximity to Coronado Springs. Unfortunately, this means that if you do not like the food options that are offered, it is not very convenient to dine at another resort restaurant.

Port Orleans Resort. There are two distinct resorts at Port Orleans – Port Orleans French Quarter and Port Orleans

Riverside. In 2012, the full-size beds are slated to be replaced with queen-size beds, which are standard in the Deluxe Resorts.

Princesses rejoice! Beginning March, 2012, princess-themed rooms will be offered at Port Orleans Riverside. Princess Tiana's friends have stayed in the royal guest rooms and left behind a token of their appreciation such as a magic carpet from Jasmine and a magical footstool from Belle. Pricing is expected to be about $30 per night higher than a standard room.

Port Orleans French Quarter is the smaller of the two resorts and captures the distinctive atmosphere of the historic French Quarter of New Orleans with its authentic details and understated elegance. For more fun, the spirit of Mardi Gras is captured particularly well by the feature pool area, Doubloon Lagoon. If you're looking for a pleasant way to spend the afternoon, take the riverboat to Downtown Disney, a 30-minute cruise down the Sassagoula River. Unfortunately, there is no table-service dining at this resort; for table-service, you'll have to go to Port Orleans Riverside, about a 15-minute walk. There is, however, a food court.

Port Orleans Riverside amazes me with the true-to-life architecture of a resort that celebrates southern living in Louisiana. The atmosphere is one of a more leisurely country life than in the "Big City" represented by Port Orleans French Quarter. There are two distinct styles of guest buildings – antebellum plantation and relaxed country cottages. The fishing hole, with catch and release fishing, completes the picture of a simpler time. The sprawling layout of this resort means you either have to take a resort bus or a potentially very long walk to get to food, shopping, and the bayou-themed feature pool.

Value Resorts

These resorts are family- and group-friendly with grounds that are generally less spacious than the grounds at the Moderate Resorts. Bus transportation is required to travel to the theme parks. The Value Resorts have fewer and larger (motel style) guest buildings than those at the Moderate Resorts; rooms are small, without a double sink and vanity, and have limited storage for clothing. The resorts can be noisy with the large number of families and tour groups that choose these budget-friendly accommodations. As expected for a Value Resort, the ratio of guests to staff is higher than resorts in a higher price category but you'll still receive the legendary Disney service.

For a standard room, rates range from $84 in Value Season to $174 per night during Holiday Season.

The Value Resorts are All-Star Movies Resort, All-Star Music Resort, All-Star Sports Resort, Art of Animation Resort, and Pop Century Resort.

Amenities. The Value Resorts contain large food courts with enough variety to satisfy the whole family. The theming of these resorts, with their larger-than-life icons, appeals to kids. A drawback is the lack of a table-service dining option.

All-Star Movies Resort. This resort celebrates Hollywood and pays homage to your favorite Disney movies. Room theming and larger-than-life icons transport you into your favorite movies, such as *101 Dalmatians*, *Fantasia*, *The Love Bug*, *The Mighty Ducks*, and *Toy Story*. The All-Star Movies Resort has two pools. The Fantasia Pool has Sorcerer Mickey spraying fountains of water into the air. The second pool, Duck Pond, is a nod to the hit movie, *The Mighty Ducks*. This pool is shaped and themed like an ice hockey rink, with Goofy as the goalie. With arcades and a food court, the Value Resorts are very similar except for theming.

All-Star Music Resort. Whether rock, jazz, or country music is your pleasure, Disney's All-Star Music Resort has lodging that will make you feel right at home. The 1,600+ rooms are divided into five musical sections: Broadway (show tunes), Calypso, Country, Jazz, and Rock 'n Roll. Like all the Value Resorts, huge icons characterize the resort's theme. This theming is carried over to the two pools, one guitar shaped and one piano shaped.

All-Star Sports Resort. The All-Star Sports Resort is perfect for the sports enthusiast. Baseball, basketball, football, surfing, and tennis are represented. There are ten guest buildings broken into five sections at the All-Star Sports, just like the rest of the Value Resorts. Guests have access to two pools, a food court, and arcade. The baseball-themed pool, Grand Slam, features Goofy operating a small water cannon.

Art of Animation Resort. Opening in summer, 2012, over half the rooms in this new resort will be family suites, sleeping six. The family suites will contain two bathrooms, a master bedroom, and a kitchenette.

Theming at this new resort will revolve around the beloved Disney and Pixar animated films, *Cars*, *Finding Nemo*, *The Lion King*, and *The Little Mermaid*.

Pop Century Resort. Most adults can relive some aspects of their childhood at this resort that features pop culture from the 1950s through the 1990s. Each decade is represented by a

different area of the resort and lodging is themed accordingly.
Oversized symbols of each decade, such as bowling pins and the
Rubik's Cube, cheerfully dominate the resort. This fun and
graphic resort has more than 2,800 guest rooms, three large
pools, and an arcade. The '50s area of the resort features a
bowling pin-shaped pool while flower power is alive and well at
the '60s-themed pool. A computer-themed pool is located
between the '80s and '90s areas of the resort.

Need More Space?

Rent. Disney's Vacation Club (DVC) Vacation Homes offer a
variety of lodging options. Choices include a Studio (most sleep
4) with a refrigerator and microwave; a one-bedroom Vacation
Home (most sleep 4) with a kitchen, washer and dryer, and
living room; a two-bedroom Vacation Home (most sleep 8) with
all the amenities of a one-bedroom Vacation Home; and a Grand
Villa (sleeps 12) with three bedrooms and bathrooms, living
room, dining room, and kitchen.

DVC members often rent their DVC points if they cannot
vacation within a particular year. Care must be taken as these
transactions do not occur through Disney and are undertaken at
your own risk. If you cancel your trip, you will likely lose your
money. Renting DVC points while you have a young family is
worth considering.

Renting a one-bedroom Vacation Home with little ones is
advantageous. Mom and Dad can unwind by reading or watching
television in a separate room without disturbing sleeping kids.
Having a full kitchen to prepare simple meals is a bonus.

DVC Resorts are Animal Kingdom Villas, Bay Lake Tower at the Contemporary Resort, Beach Club Villas, Boardwalk Villas, Old Key West Villas, Saratoga Springs Resort & Spa, Treehouse Villas at Saratoga Springs Resort & Spa, and Villas at Disney's Wilderness Lodge.

 You can rent DVC points at the DISboards DVC Rent/Trade forum and MouseOwners.com's Rent/Trade/Transfer Board. Expect to pay between $8-12 per point. For a more secure option, consider using a broker, such as www.dvcrequest.com, which carries a higher cost.

Family Suites. Disney's All-Star Music Resort offers family suites starting at $198 per night. These more spacious accommodations sleep six and include a kitchenette with a sink, microwave, and small refrigerator, in addition to two bathrooms and a separate master bedroom.

The Art of Animation Resort, expected to open in summer 2012, will feature over one thousand family suites.

Cabins. The Cabins at Fort Wilderness Lodge sleep six and include one bedroom, one bathroom, a full kitchen, a living area, and a patio. Rates start at $285 per night.

 If you stay in lodging with a separate bedroom or read on the balcony while your toddlers fall asleep, pack a baby monitor.

3   Transportation

Getting There

Air Travel

 Take advantage of the time in the terminal prior to your flight to tire the kids out. Keep them moving by exploring the terminal and gift shops until your plane boards. There will be plenty of time to sit and rest on the flight.

Critical Supplies. Admittedly, one of my worst fears is to be stranded either in the airport or on an airplane with a small child, which unfortunately is not so unusual these days. I bring 24-hours' worth of critical supplies in my carry-on. This includes diapers/pull-ups/wipes, small meals and snacks, medications, my child's "lovey" (comfort item), a change of clothes, toys, etc.

 Don't forget to attach a gift tag to teddy bear so he can find his way home if he gets temporarily misplaced.

 If your child suffers from ear pain during flying, consider EarPlanes®. EarPlanes claim to relieve air pressure discomfort during flights.

 CARES, the Child Aviation Restraint System, is a harness-type safety restraint that has been approved by the FAA for small children in lieu of a car seat. Plan a dry run at home so you feel comfortable attaching it and your child knows what to expect during the flight. If you want to bring your own car seat on the airplane, look into a product like Go-Go Kidz Travelmate which turns your car seat into a stroller for easy wheeling through the airport.

Travel Backpacks. Allowing your children to select the toys and snacks to bring in their carry-ons can help avoid issues of "I didn't want that toy!" Help keep packing in check by reminding your children that they'll have to carry their backpacks through the airport.

Magical Express. Walt Disney World offers complimentary round-trip transportation from the Orlando International Airport to Walt Disney World resorts for on-site guests flying on participating airlines. The true benefit is that you can deplane and board your transportation without having to pick up your luggage from baggage claim. Not having to juggle kids, luggage, carry-ons, and strollers all at once is a relief. The Magical Express team will ensure the luggage is delivered directly to your resort room. It may take 3-5 hours from check-in to receive your luggage so be sure you have everything you and your child will need immediately in your carry-on.

 Car seats must be stowed under the Magical Express and cannot be installed on the bus.

On the return trip, participating airlines allow you to check your baggage directly at your Walt Disney World resort; if your airline does not participate, bring your luggage aboard the Magical Express bus.

You must make an advance reservation for the Magical Express; call 407-WDW-MAGIC.

TIP If your flight arrives between 10 p.m. and 5 a.m., the baggage claim and delivery service will not be available. You can still take advantage of the complimentary transportation; simply pick up your bags from baggage claim and bring them with you on the Magical Express.

Entertainment

Electronics. There are many affordable DVD players available. This portable electronic device is great for both air and car travel to help pass the time for your children.

Download movies or animated shorts to an iPod.

Toys. A visit to your local toy store will pay off very quickly during your travels. Purchase a variety of small, inexpensive toys that can be handed to your children throughout the trip. Perhaps they'll get a new toy every time you cross state lines or every 30 minutes on the airplane. The key is to make sure the toys are new ones they've never seen before.

Games. Card games are a great way to pass the time – they are inexpensive and easy to pack. Besides standard cards, specialized Go Fish cards and Uno for Kids are great options. Consider a game of I Spy in the airport, airplane, or car.

Getting Around the "World"

One of the benefits of staying at a Disney World resort is the free transportation provided. Bus transportation is the most prevalent, by far. Other transportation includes the monorail system and boat launches. Buses generally run every 15-20 minutes, during operating hours, from the resorts to theme parks, water parks, and Downtown Disney. Buses do not run from resort to resort. This is an important consideration when making dining reservations – it may take you upwards of an hour to travel from your resort to dinner at another resort using Disney transportation. On these occasions, consider calling a taxi.

 If you're staying at the Disney Boardwalk area hotels, the buses often make multiple stops at nearby resorts including the Walt Disney World Swan and Dolphin Resort. When returning from the theme parks, it is sometimes quicker to exit the bus at either the Swan or Dolphin and walk to your resort using the bridge to the Boardwalk.

 The Polynesian Resort is adjacent to the Transportation and Ticket Center (TTC), which has monorail service directly to Epcot. If you are traveling from this resort to Epcot, consider walking through the beautifully landscaped grounds to the TTC instead of taking the Magic Kingdom monorail from the Polynesian Resort to the TTC and transferring to the Epcot monorail.

Resort Boat Transportation

If you're looking for a distraction for your child, a short round-trip boat ride may be just the thing to try. You do not have to take kids out of strollers to board most resort boats.

Boardwalk Area to Epcot. Boats provide transportation for the short trip from the Boardwalk Inn and Villas, the Walt Disney World Swan and Dolphin Resort, Beach Club, and Yacht Club to Epcot.

Epcot's World Showcase. A short boat ride offers transportation from one side of the World Showcase to docks on the other side. This provides a shaded, relaxing alternative to walking around the World Showcase Lagoon. Boats depart from the area of World Showcase accessed directly from the Future World walkway and dock at both the Germany and Morocco Pavilions.

Magic Kingdom. Boat and ferry transportation are provided to the Magic Kingdom from Fort Wilderness Resort, Grand Floridian Resort, Polynesian Resort, Transportation and Ticket Center, and Wilderness Lodge.

The Liberty Belle Riverboat offers a nice, leisurely break from touring the parks. This approximately 20-minute cruise departs and returns to Magic Kingdom's Liberty Square.

Hollywood Studios. Disney provides boat transportation to and from Disney's Hollywood Studios from the Boardwalk Inn and Villas, the Walt Disney World Swan and Dolphin Resort, Beach Club, and Yacht Club.

Downtown Disney. Boats provide transportation between Old Key West, Saratoga Springs, and Port Orleans Resort and Downtown Disney.

Fort Wilderness Resort. From Fort Wilderness Resort, you may enjoy a water launch to the Magic Kingdom, Wilderness Lodge, or the Contemporary Resort.

4   Touring

Touring is the approach you take to experiencing the Walt Disney World theme parks. You'll have to decide which theme parks you'll visit and how many days you'll spend at each one. Once you're at the theme parks, will you go "commando" and hit all the major attractions without stopping or will you take a more leisurely approach to touring? Here is what you should know to improve your touring experience.

Best Preschooler Theme Parks

Hands down, the Magic Kingdom is the most preschooler-friendly park and families should plan on spending at least two days there; this provides enough opportunity to experience the headliner attractions at a moderate pace while enjoying an afternoon rest period.

The second best park for preschoolers is a toss-up between Animal Kingdom and Disney's Hollywood Studios. If your preschoolers love animals, my pick would be Animal Kingdom. The wonderful stage shows, inventive playground, and ample opportunities to view animals put it over the top. If your child is a huge fan of Disney Junior and the Little Mermaid, Disney's Hollywood Studios may your child's second favorite park. Disney's Hollywood Studios features more shows than rides for preschoolers; it also has a unique playground.

Epcot is often overlooked as a theme park for small children and it is a shame. Although it wouldn't be the first Walt Disney World theme park I would recommend for preschoolers, it is worth a visit if you have more than four days to visit the theme parks, especially if your little ones are more adventurous and want to try the headliner attractions, Soarin', and Test Track. The pathways are wider and this park is often less-crowded than other Disney World parks. Another benefit is the Character Greetings in World Showcase which feature popular characters with shorter waits than at Magic Kingdom. The Winter Holidays and the Flower and Garden Festival in the spring are great times to introduce kids to Epcot.

Planning your Days at Walt Disney World

Extra Magic Hours. A perk available to Walt Disney World resort guests is Extra Magic Hours (EMH). See Chapter 2, "Disney Lodging," for more information.

Whether guests should visit the park with the morning EMH is a subject of much debate in the Disney community; I am of the opinion that it makes sense with small children. Taking advantage of the morning EMH will allow you to visit the parks while you're rested, the weather is cooler, and the crowds are thinner. Also, my kids are up at the crack of dawn so it doesn't make sense to hang around a hotel room when we could be touring. Those who advocate skipping the park with the morning EMH argue that it becomes more crowded since Disney guests flock to this park; I have never found it overly crowded on EMH mornings although it does fill up by midday – just when we're leaving to take an afternoon break. When booking any character breakfasts, select a day when your family is not interested in taking advantage of the morning EMH.

If you are night owls and decide to sleep late, have a leisurely brunch, and get in some pool time before going to the parks, keep in mind that the quantity of FASTPASS tickets is limited. For the most popular rides, they may be completely distributed by midday. When arriving at the parks later in the day, consider visiting a park that does not offer Extra Magic Hours; the theme parks offering regular hours will usually be less crowded.

 Not all attractions and restaurants open early/stay open late during the Extra Magic Hours. Visit the Walt Disney World website (www.disneyworld.com) for a current list of attractions that participate. This list is also available from the theme parks and Walt Disney World resorts.

Park Calendar. Park opening and closing hours vary by season, special events, etc. The park hours, including Extra Magic Hours, for the Walt Disney World theme parks are available at www.disneyworld.com, approximately 180 days in advance.

 Park entry is required to eat at theme park restaurants. If you don't have the Park Hopper Option on your tickets, first plan which parks you'll be visiting on which days. Then, make your dining reservations based on the theme park you are visiting that day.

Game Plan. Before you visit, research attraction height requirements. There's nothing worse than looks of disappointment (or worse) when being turned away from a ride your kids have been looking forward to all vacation. See Chapter 5, "Attractions," for a list of current height requirements. Familiarize yourself with the park layout and the attractions your children will most likely enjoy – you'll be able to get more out of your days at the parks if you have a game plan going in.

Rest Periods and Pool Time. It's very easy to succumb to the temptation to experience just one more ride or see one more show. After all, Disney vacations can be expensive and it may be years before you find yourself back on Disney property. Remind yourself of the exhausted children (or adults, for that matter) you see having a meltdown in the middle of the Magic Kingdom's Main Street, U.S.A. Of course, a preschooler being a preschooler, your child may just have a meltdown anyway. You can help your child enjoy the vacation more by scheduling daily rest periods and downtime. Going back to the room for a nap, a movie, or some pool time is a great way to break up a busy day. After everyone is rested, return to the theme parks for a few hours in the late afternoon/early evening. Consider your child's schedule and what will work best for all of you.

Switch It Up. For my children, too many rides in a row can cause some less than desirable behavior. We try to enjoy a ride or two and then have a snack break, take in an air-conditioned show, or visit a playground to blow off some steam before enjoying more rides. As much as I advocate planning for your Walt Disney World vacation, I've found that being flexible and sometimes deviating from the plan is critical to a successful trip with preschoolers.

Reducing Wait Time

Touring Plans. Different Disney websites sell theme park itineraries that are designed to minimize your attraction wait time. A few of these sites are Tour Guide Mike (www.tourguidemike.com), Touring Plans (www.touringplans.com), and RideMax (www.ridemax.com).

Lines, a mobile website available on a wide variety of mobile devices, has received rave reviews. The Unofficial Guide team (www.touringplans.com) harness years of wait-time data to predict current wait times and anticipated wait times for later in the day. You can even use Lines to get an attraction's current FASTPASS return time.

Reducing the time you wait in lines will undoubtedly improve your Disney experience. Take advantage of some of Disney World's existing policies.

FASTPASS. FASTPASS is an indispensible service available to all Disney World ticket holders. Simply put, a FASTPASS is a ticket that allows you to return to the attraction later in the day and skip the regular (standby) line. Using the much shorter FASTPASS line will dramatically reduce your wait time. At the entrance of each attraction, the current FASTPASS return window is displayed; the return window is one hour. If you decide to print a FASTPASS by inserting your theme park ticket in the FASTPASS machine, the ticket will have the return window and the time you are eligible to get another FASTPASS. Return during the time period printed on your FASTPASS and use the attraction's FASTPASS entrance.

 If you return after your FASTPASS return window closes, you will still be able to use the FASTPASS.

Sample Strategy. My family visits a popular attraction as soon as the park opens and before the lines build. Even more effective is visiting a ride where long lines build early and no FASTPASS is offered (such as Dumbo the Flying Elephant in the Magic Kingdom). When we exit the attraction, we get a FASTPASS. While we wait for the FASTPASS window to open, we'll visit other non-FASTPASS attractions. We repeat this process throughout the day.

 TIP All ticket holders don't have to be present to get a FASTPASS. One parent can take the tickets and get a FASTPASS for everyone in the family while the other takes the kids on a ride.

See "FASTPASS Attractions" for a list of attractions that offer FASTPASS.

Wait Times. Each Walt Disney World theme park has a Tip Board, in a central location, which lists the current wait times for the most popular park attractions. If possible, visit these boards several times a day to make the most of your limited touring time. For locations, look for the large 'T' on your park map.

Single Rider Line. Two rides, Test Track in Epcot and Rock 'n' Roller Coaster in Hollywood Studios, offer a single-rider line that is usually significantly shorter than the standby line. Multiple persons in your party can use this line at one time – you just won't be able to sit together. Check your park map for the 'S' symbol.

Rider Swap Policy. Attractions with height restrictions offer a Rider Swap option. This allows members of your travel group to ride the attraction while a parent stays with a child who cannot ride. Once one parent exits the ride and swaps roles, the adult who initially stayed behind can ride the attraction with minimal wait. Just let the Cast Member know you are interested in Rider Swap and you'll be handed a FASTPASS that is good for three people. This Rider Swap FASTPASS will not affect your ability to get another FASTPASS using your park admission.

Entertaining the Kids While on Line

Facts are facts. You may be Supermom but you have yet to
master the art of altering the time-space continuum. That means
your little one will have to spend some time waiting on line for
attractions. Luckily, Disney World has been updating some of its
queues to be more interactive. The best example of this for
parents of preschoolers is the Many Adventures of Winnie the
Pooh queue. Kids can spring like Tigger, play with vegetables
that double as musical instruments, wake up some gophers, and
create magic on a "hunny" wall.

Plan Your Next Move. Review park maps with your kids while
on line. Decide which attraction to visit next.

Shutterbugs. Purchase an inexpensive, disposable camera and
your preschoolers can take pictures of the attraction queues and
the family. As out of focus as they may be, the photographs will
be a great way to remember the trip – through your kids' eyes.

Bubbles and Stickers. I don't know many preschoolers who
don't love bubbles and stickers. If you don't mind your t-shirt
being a blank slate for your child's stickers, you don't even need
paper or an activity book.

Refuel. Waiting on line is a great time to make sure your kids
are fed and hydrated. Eating small, dry snacks like Animal
Crackers® and Goldfish® will keep them busy and satisfied.

Activity Books. Activity books with hidden pictures or connect-
the-dots are inexpensive and portable.

Small Toys. Look for travel editions of popular toys such as
Etch A Sketch®, Aquadoodle, and inexpensive handheld games.

Game Systems. My son will entertain himself for quite some time with his Nintendo DS.

iPod/iPhone. If you feel comfortable letting your little ones use your electronics, you can download videos and Disney-related apps to entertain them while waiting.

Strollers

Rentals. Disney-designed strollers can be rented near the entrance of each Disney theme park and at other select park locations either daily or for the length of your stay. Rentals are $15 per day for a single stroller and $31 per day for a double. There is a small savings for a length-of-stay rental of about $2 per day for a single and $4 per day for a double stroller. Prices are subject to change so check with Walt Disney World prior to your visit. If you rent a length-of-stay stroller, you will receive a voucher for each day of your visit. With these vouchers in hand, bypass the rental line and proceed directly to the stroller pickup area.

The strollers must be returned at each park entrance or a rental location within the park and cannot be brought back to your resort. Additionally, they are made of hard plastic and do not recline. For these reasons, I like to bring my own stroller (make sure it has a large canopy for shade) or rent from an Orlando-based company. It helps to know that I can leave the park with my tired or sleeping child in the stroller without having to carry him from the park exit to the transportation back to the resort. At many resorts, there is quite a distance between guest rooms and the transportation areas; a personal stroller helps cover this distance more quickly and easily.

Umbrella strollers may be purchased in some gift shops for $50.

Strollers may also be rented from Orlando Stroller Rentals. The biggest benefit? You'll be able to use the strollers in the parks, at your resort, and anywhere else you go in Orlando. These strollers offer a large canopy for shade, are very maneuverable, and are very comfortable for your kids. Rental companies will deliver the stroller to your resort upon check-in and will pick it up at the end of your stay. This is also a nice option if you have more than one small child and do not own a double stroller; a child as old as five will benefit from a stroller throughout a long day at Walt Disney World.

Stroller Parking. When designing a theme park, who would have thought to have designated areas for strollers to be parked? Disney did! This small detail has a big impact. All guests benefit from orderly walkways and do not have to navigate an obstacle course filled with errant strollers; parents can relax knowing exactly where to leave their stroller. Cast Members attend to the stroller parking areas and ensure the space is neat and tidy. Please be aware that Cast Members may move your stroller within the stroller parking area in an effort to efficiently use the available space.

Just as you mark your suitcase with some identifying feature when you travel on an airplane, it will be helpful to mark your stroller. Many strollers are similar and using ribbon or a luggage tag will make it easy for you to not only identify it as your own but to prevent others from mistakenly taking it.

 Be Strategic. Consider parking your stroller in a location central to a few attractions you plan on visiting. With the sheer volume of strollers at Walt

Disney World, it can be a challenge to retrieve your stroller after each attraction.

Baby Care Centers

The Baby Care Centers are an amazing resource for families with young children. They contain a nursing room; some have restrooms with child-sized toilets that do not have automatic flushers; changing tables; and an area in which to feed children, complete with high-chairs, bottle warmers, and more.

Most Baby Care Centers have a wide variety of baby supplies for purchase. These include baby/junior food, juice, sippy cups, bottles, nipples, pacifiers, diapers, diaper ointment, and children's over-the-counter medications.

Magic Kingdom. The Magic Kingdom Baby Care Center is located next to Casey's Corner and the Crystal Palace Restaurant on Main Street, U.S.A.

Epcot. The Epcot Baby Care Center is in the Odyssey Center, located in Future World, on the bridge between Test Track and the World Showcase's Mexico Pavilion. This Baby Care Center does not have pint-sized toilets.

Disney Hollywood Studios. The Hollywood Studios Baby Care Center is located directly inside the park entrance. It is in the same building that houses Guest Services. This Baby Care Center doesn't carry baby supplies.

Animal Kingdom. The Animal Kingdom Baby Care Center is next to Creature Comforts in Africa. It is near the junction of

Discovery Island and Africa. This location does not have smaller toilets for little ones.

Enhancing Your Experience

The following services are available to Walt Disney World guests and can "plus up" your visit.

Package Delivery. It can be a daunting task to carry all your souvenirs through the theme parks during a long day of touring. Disney offers a wonderfully convenient service to Walt Disney World resort guests. If you are not checking out of the resort immediately, have the package sent from the theme park gift shop to your resort where you can pick it up once you get back to your resort. If you are not staying on Disney property or will be checking out soon, not to worry. Packages can also be delivered to the Guest Relations location at the front of the theme park. Stop and pick up your packages as you exit the park.

Lockers. Disney theme parks offer daily locker rentals for $7 per day with a $5 key deposit. The locker rental locations are indicated on each park map and are conveniently located close to the park entrance. If you park hop, you can use your locker rental receipt to rent a locker at another park without additional fees.

PhotoPass. Disney PhotoPass photographers can be found throughout the Disney theme parks and will happily capture your family's vacation moments. Just hand them your free PhotoPass card. The photographers carry these cards; pick one up at your first PhotoPass location. If your family splits up at the park, simply get additional PhotoPass cards. More than one card can be linked to a single account on the Disney PhotoPass website. The PhotoPass photographers take pictures at no charge and the digital photographs will be available for purchase online for 30 days from the date they were taken. The photographers will even take your photo with your own camera if you ask.

 Copy your PhotoPass card number on a piece of paper, or even take a picture with a cell phone or digital camera, and store it in a safe place during your stay. If you misplace your PhotoPass card, you will still be able to claim your photographs with the PhotoPass number.

Your family and friends can view your favorite vacation moments and also order prints, a PhotoCD, and other specialty products from the Disney PhotoPass website.

 A preorder discount of $50 on a PhotoPass PhotoCD is commonly available at www.disneyphotopass.com/previsitoffer.aspx.

You may also view and order photographs at a Disney PhotoPass center at the Walt Disney World Resort. Ask for locations at each theme park's Guest Relations.

 Stop at a Disney PhotoPass center to add a photograph you purchased from a character dining experience to your Disney PhotoPass card; receipt required.

Mobile Magic. Walt Disney World has partnered with Verizon and provides Verizon customers with park updates such as Character Greeting locations, attraction availability, parade times, and more on their mobile phone. The app is free from the Verizon Media Store or by texting MAGIC to 2777 (message and data rates apply).

Lost and Found. The number of lost items that the Walt Disney World Resort's Lost and Found catalogs is staggering. To inquire about a lost item, call 407-824-4245.

Potty Training. Consistency in potty-training can be a challenge with the excitement of Disney World. To further complicate matters, your children may be frightened by the automatic toilet flushers in restrooms. If this is the case, try the child-friendly toilets in the Baby Care Centers at Magic Kingdom or Disney's Hollywood Studios. Not only are these toilets smaller in size than the ones throughout the theme park, they also do not have automatic flushers.

Post-its. Post-its are lightweight, inexpensive, and easy to carry. Use Post-its to cover automatic flushers and prevent flushing before you're ready.

The theme parks also have Companion Restrooms that are larger in size. These can be useful if a caregiver of the opposite sex needs to help a child use the restroom. Please be aware that these restrooms are limited and may be the only ones that guests with physical disabilities can comfortably use.

Baby changing stations are available in Walt Disney World restrooms, even the men's rooms.

Rainy Days

Rain can put a damper on any vacation. Luckily, there are many different things families can take advantage of during a rainy day at the Walt Disney World Resort.

Ride the Attractions. Rain at Walt Disney World offers a unique opportunity for your family to have the theme parks practically to yourselves. Armed with ponchos and a positive attitude, enjoy the most popular attractions with a minimal wait.

Epcot and Hollywood Studios are your best bets during inclement weather. Both parks either have structures that hold multiple attractions or longer-running shows that allow you to spend more time indoors.

In Epcot, check out The Land Pavilion, The Seas with Nemo & Friends Pavilion, and Innoventions. The Land Pavilion offers a quality food court with many healthy options, The Circle of Life, and Living with the Land, all under one roof. After enjoying The Seas with Nemo & Friends, and Turtle Talk with Crush (in The Seas with Nemo & Friends Pavilion), take some time to explore the aquarium. Innoventions features rotating exhibits of the latest products and technologies; there are a lot of opportunities for hands-on fun.

Preschooler-friendly shows at Hollywood Studios include Muppet Vision 3D, Voyage of the Little Mermaid, Disney Junior-Live on Stage, and Beauty and the Beast-Live on Stage.

So, what can you do if you're in the Magic Kingdom or Animal Kingdom? For a short summer cloudburst in the Magic Kingdom, try hopping on the Walt Disney World Railroad or the Tomorrowland Transit Authority PeopleMover or visit Walt Disney's Carousel of Progress in Tomorrowland. Duck into Pinocchio Village Haus for a bite to eat. Many rides in Magic Kingdom, particularly Fantasyland, are close together but the rides themselves are short. If you're in Animal Kingdom, you won't have much choice but to make the best of it.

If the forecast calls for rain, consider bringing quick-drying footwear to slip on when the rain begins. After the rain, put your walking shoes back on.

Resort Hop. Hop on a bus or monorail to explore different Disney resorts. Stroll around the lobby and take in the detail-rich theming and ambience of the resort. Visit the gift shops, eat lunch, or encourage your kids to participate in an arts and crafts activity. Look for Hidden Mickeys at the resort. See Chapter 6, "Hidden Activities," for more information on Hidden Mickeys.

Game Time. When it rains, head to your Disney resort's arcade and prove to your kids that Mom and Dad still have some game.

Take in a Movie. Take a bus to Downtown Disney and enjoy an afternoon movie.

Downtown Disney. Downtown Disney offers a wide variety of shopping and dining opportunities.

Take a Nap. Last but not least, rain provides a wonderful opportunity to enjoy a guilt-free nap and recharge your batteries.

5   Attractions

Preschooler-Friendly Attractions

The following attractions are preschooler-friendly. This list is intended to be a starting point for your planning; as always, your child's interests, fears, and personality should be taken into account. See "Maps" for a map of each theme park.

 When you arrive at each Disney theme park, visit Guest Relations for a kid-centric park map that highlights where you can find characters, attractions, and activities suitable for young children.

 Disney advises expectant mothers not to ride these preschooler-friendly attractions.

 The wait for these popular attractions increases quickly. Visit early or get a FASTPASS if one is offered.

Magic Kingdom

Walt Disney World is undertaking a major expansion that will double the size of Fantasyland. Dubbed the New Fantasyland, the Fantasyland Expansion will be rolled out in phases beginning in late 2012. Unfortunately, a project of this size will affect existing attractions; some attractions will be moved and others will be closed. As of this printing, all dates have not been announced and some of the Magic Kingdom attractions may be temporarily or permanently closed during your visit. Updates will be posted at www.BeyondTheAttractions.com as they are received.

⚠ **The Barnstormer** (Fantasyland). Formerly The Barnstormer at Goofy's Wiseacre Farm, this mini roller coaster will be hosted by the Great Goofini and re-themed to fit with the nearby Storybook Circus. It is a perfect introduction to thrill rides for more adventurous children. There are no loops, just speed and tight turns on this approximately one-minute coaster that parents can ride with their kids. This ride will most likely not reopen until late 2012.

Buzz Lightyear's Space Ranger Spin (Tomorrowland). This delightful ride is addictive for children and adults alike. Board your space cruiser and try to outscore your opponent by hitting the brightly colored targets with your laser cannon. Smaller children may have difficulty aiming at the targets during this moving ride.

Captain Jack Sparrow's Pirate Tutorial (Adventureland). This popular street show will school your kids in the finer points of pirate swordplay and teach them the requisite pirate song, "Yo Ho (A Pirate's Life for Me)."

Country Bear Jamboree (Frontierland). This animatronics musical revue is popular with the preschool crowd and features folksy songs and corny jokes performed by a variety of easygoing country bears.

Dream Along with Mickey (Fantasyland). This Cinderella Castle stage show features Mickey and friends reminding guests that dreams do come true. Disney princesses and pirates help to

tell this musical story. There will be some surprise guests and
fireworks.

Dumbo the Flying Elephant (Fantasyland). Be prepared
for long lines on this Walt Disney World favorite. Climb aboard
your favorite flying elephant and slowly soar in a circle. Riders
are able to control how high their ride vehicle ascends. This ride
is expected to be closed sometime in 2012 as work begins for its
move to Storybook Circus. Storybook Circus, with its interactive
wait area and circus theme, will feature dueling Dumbos, a water
play area, and The Barnstormer mini roller coaster.

Enchanted Tales with Belle (Fantasyland). As part of a *Beauty
and the Beast* area in the New Fantasyland that includes the Be
Our Guest restaurant and Belle's village, the "story as old as
time" will be retold. Guests will be magically transported from
Maurice's workshop to the Beast's library for this interactive
experience. This attraction will likely open in fall 2012.

"it's a small world" (Fantasyland). Children and adults alike
will be humming the catchy tune from this ride that uses
costumed dolls to celebrate different countries and cultures while
embracing humanity's similarities. This classic attraction was
refurbished in recent years, making it even more fanciful.

Jungle Cruise (Adventureland). Silly jokes abound on this
piloted cruise through a jungle; snakes, hippos, and elephants are
just some of the animatronic animals that call these rivers home.
Your enjoyment of this ride will depend in large part on how
entertaining your Cast Member is.

Mad Tea Party (Fantasyland). Spinning … dizzy … spinning … dizzier … spinning … dizziest. That pretty much sums up the Mad Tea Party as guests take a whirl in spinning tea cups based on Alice in Wonderland's Unbirthday Party scene. Riders can control how quickly the tea cup spins with a wheel in the center. I recommend this attraction with reservations; even if your kids can handle the spinning, you may not!

The Magic Carpets of Aladdin (Adventureland). Who hasn't wanted to glide high above the world on a magic carpet? This attraction is similar to the Flying Dumbo ride. Park guests board whimsical magic carpets, which seat four, and take a flying journey around a genie bottle. Riders in the front control the up and down motion while rear riders can change the pitch of the ride vehicle. Beware the spitting camel.

The Many Adventures of Winnie the Pooh (Fantasyland). The new interactive queue designed to captivate Disney's youngest guests is almost an attraction in itself. And the main event doesn't disappoint: gentle bounces, special effects, and a hint of danger elevate this popular attraction from a mere trip through the pages of a classic Winnie the Pooh story to a memorable journey. Your ride vehicle is a Hunny Pot. Young, sensitive children may be uncomfortable with the stormy scene.

Mickey's PhilharMagic (Fantasyland). The whole family will delight in this 3-D journey through popular Disney animated films such as *Fantasia, Beauty and the Beast, The Lion King, The Little Mermaid,* and *Aladdin.* The movie scenes come alive with the addition of scents and other special effects.

TIP   The Disney 3-D shows are still enjoyable if your preschooler refuses to wear the 3-D glasses.

Monsters, Inc. Laugh Floor (Tomorrowland). This Disney attraction, with a *Monsters, Inc.* theme, will appeal more to older preschoolers than toddlers. Your favorite monsters need to power their world using laughter; be prepared to laugh out loud at the many corny jokes. Guests have the opportunity to text jokes and your children will be thrilled if their jokes are selected.

Peter Pan's Flight (Fantasyland). This Walt Disney World favorite takes you on a journey through the classic story of Peter Pan. Board sailing ships and swoop over historic London at night as you make your way to Never Land. You'll see that Peter defeats the no-good Captain Hook and frees the Darling children from the pirate's wicked clutches.

Prince Charming Regal Carrousel (Fantasyland). This classic ride hearkens back to days gone by. Children will enjoy riding the horses on this traditional and beautifully detailed carousel. See if your family can figure out which horse is Cinderella's.

Princess Fairytale Hall (Fantasyland). The princesses will move into a regal new hall to receive visitors as part of the New Fantasyland. Aurora, Cinderella, and Tiana are expected to greet their friends beginning in fall 2013.

Seven Dwarfs Mine Train (Fantasyland). Here's a sneak peek at an attraction that will debut in early 2014 as part of the New Fantasyland. Scenes from the beloved fairy tale *Snow White* will be depicted in this mildly thrilling ride that features mine carts with a unique side-to-side swaying motion and songs from this classic story.

Shrunken Ned's Junior Jungle Boats (Adventureland). This often-overlooked mini-attraction is next to Jungle Cruise. For

se, your family can test their skills at piloting
ʒions of the Jungle Cruise boats through a small
ɔr spears.

Tom Sawyer Island (Frontierland). This large play area has
many interesting activities for the pre-K crowd, from exploring
caves and mines to walking over barrel bridges. It's a great way
for your children to have some freedom to run and investigate.

Tomorrowland Speedway (Tomorrowland). Drive a
"racecar" along a racecourse complete with turns; cars run along
a track so youngsters steering the vehicle won't go too far astray.
This behind-the-wheel driving experience may be tedious for
adults with the slow speed of the ride vehicles, the engines'
exhaust, and the long waits, but kids tend to love this one.

Tomorrowland Transit Authority PeopleMover
(Tomorrowland). This relaxing ride is a must-do for my family
on every Walt Disney World trip. When you need a break from
the heat, crowds, and tired feet, hop on for an approximately ten-
minute tour of Tomorrowland. The elevated ride takes you past
windows that offer a glimpse into Space Mountain and Buzz
Lightyear's Space Ranger Spin.

Town Square Theater (Main Street, U.S.A.) The big cheese
himself (that would be Mickey Mouse) and Minnie Mouse have
moved to their new digs in Town Square Theater. Guests have
the opportunity to go "backstage" to meet this famous couple.
While the princesses wait to move into their new Princess
Fairytale Hall, they'll be meeting their subjects here also.

Under the Sea – Journey of the Little Mermaid (Fantasyland).
Ariel is getting her own dark ride, which is expected to be

completed in fall 2012. New animatronic technology will make Ariel more realistic than ever, including hair that bobs and sways "underwater." Clamshells will transport guests from land to under the seas through the musical retelling of the popular animated feature, *The Little Mermaid*.

Walt Disney World Railroad (Main Street, U.S.A.; Frontierland). Not only is this ride a convenient means to traverse the Magic Kingdom theme park with its two stations, it's also a great way to sit back, relax, and people-watch during your busy day at the park.

TIP   Have your child ask to sit in the back seat and yell, "All Aboard!" Honorary conductors receive a small certificate.

Epcot

The Circle of Life (The Land). This humorous, yet educational, film starring *The Lion King*'s Simba, Pumbaa, and Timon, teaches about both the dangers of environmental pollution and the benefits of conservation. Pumbaa and Timon's dreams of building a luxury resort are dashed as Simba opens their eyes to the effects this development would have on the rest of the animals living on the savannah.

Epcot Character Spot (Innoventions West). Mickey and his friends now have a permanent greeting location. Be sure to have those autograph books and smiles ready.

Gran Fiesta Tour Starring the Three Caballeros (World Showcase; Mexico). This slow-moving boat ride is a relaxing way to celebrate the culture of Mexico with the help of "The Three Caballeros." Donald Duck is missing and his two

amigos must find their sightseeing friend in time for their big
show.

ImageWorks – The Kodak "What If" Labs (Imagination!).
This interactive area entertains children with its hands-on
activities. Create music with your body's motion or customize
your own Figment.

Journey into Imagination with Figment (Imagination!).
Figment is your enthusiastic guide through this fun-filled (for
preschoolers) ride highlighting the senses and the imagination.
Adults may have to feign interest on this attraction. The loud
sound and flash of light after exiting Figment's upside-down
house may startle small children.

Kidcot Fun Stops (World Showcase). The eleven countries
featured in Epcot's World Showcase have Kidcot Fun Stops for
your little ones. At each Kidcot station, Cast Members will
stamp your child's free Kidcot mask, which can be picked up at
the first country you visit. Kids are encouraged to decorate their
Kidcot mask by participating in arts and crafts at each country.
Cast Members may sign the mask in their native language and
teach your toddlers and preschoolers a little about the culture of
the country they are "visiting."

Living with the Land (The Land). After boarding a slow-
moving boat, guests will learn about food production and receive
a behind-the-scenes look at some of the latest research and
advances in agriculture and aquaculture. Visitors will also see
some of the very food they enjoy at the Walt Disney World
restaurants at this working "farm." Although this is not a ride
you would traditionally think of for children, there are enough

interesting things for them to see; your whole family will enjoy this attraction.

Maelstrom (World Showcase; Norway). Older preschoolers are more likely to enjoy the thrills and excitement of this Viking voyage through Norway's past and present. You'll meet trolls, traverse Norwegian fjords, and be awed by polar bears. Please be cautioned that although the ride itself is not very intense, it does contain some unexpected drops and the theming may be frightening for smaller children.

The Seas with Nemo & Friends (The Seas with Nemo & Friends). After boarding your Clamobile, this ride takes you on an underwater pursuit of everyone's favorite clownfish, Nemo, using Disney animation. As you slowly descend to the pavilion's lower floor, follow Nemo and his friends as they explore their underwater playground, complete with real marine life. After the attraction, be sure to spend some time enjoying the aquarium.

Turtle Talk with Crush (The Seas with Nemo & Friends). This popular attraction is not to be missed. The Disney team has utilized technology that enables Crush, from *Finding Nemo*, to interact with the audience in real-time. Crush will ask questions and engage young audience members, all the while responding to what they say. No two shows will ever be the same. Little ones as well as adults will be delighted and amazed.

Hollywood Studios

Beauty and the Beast (Sunset Boulevard). This live stage show in a covered outdoor theater recreates Disney's beloved *Beauty and the Beast*. The elaborate musical production's wardrobe and set designs do not disappoint.

⏰   **Disney Junior–Live on Stage!** (Animation Courtyard). This children's show features favorite shows from Disney Junior such as "Mickey Mouse Clubhouse," "Handy Manny," "Jake and the Never Land Pirate," and "Little Einsteins." Kids have lots of opportunities to participate in the fun with clapping, dancing, and shouting. Don't miss this one.

"Honey, I Shrunk the Kids" Movie Set Adventure (Streets of America). This playground is nothing like you'd find in your local neighborhood park. Children enter the world of the miniaturized Szalinkski children; they will climb on larger-than-life spider webs and slide down enormous leaves and blades of grass.

⏰   **Jedi Training Academy** (Echo Lake). If your preschooler is a fan of the *Star Wars* movies, this attraction could be the highlight of the trip. Young Jedi Padawans (ages 4-12) are pre-selected to first train as a Jedi and then defeat Darth Vader. The Cast Members are outstanding in working with the kids and successfully including them in the training activities. Visit a Cast Member at Sounds Dangerous as soon as you enter the park at rope drop to sign your child up for a show; available slots often fill up in the first hour. Your child must be present to sign-up. Once a show is filled, Cast Members begin filling the next one.

Lights, Motors, Action! Extreme Stunt Show (Streets of America). Older preschoolers will enjoy this live show which includes a guest appearance by Lightning McQueen, especially if they're interested in action and cars. This stunt show presents a behind-the-scenes look at how car chases in your favorite movies are created and controlled. Think about skipping this one if your child is scared by intense stunts or explosions.

Muppet Vision 3D (Streets of America). Children and adults will enjoy this funny, 3-D attraction featuring your favorite Muppet characters. Kermit begins to take you on a tour of Muppet Labs when Waldo, a prototype 3-D graphic, escapes from the lab and causes mischief, to the amusement of the audience. Meanwhile, Miss Piggy is quintessential Miss Piggy. This is a must-see with little ones.

Phineas & Ferb: We're Making a Movie (Streets of America). This play-and-greet experience combines the traditional character meet and greet with a short show. The director involves young guests in recreating scenes from Phineas & Ferb episodes while the famous duo meet their fans and provide autographs.

 Toy Story Mania! (Pixar Place). This wildly popular attraction takes you through the world of classic carnival games, with a *Toy Story* theme of course! Riders don 3-D glasses and use "cannons" to aim at targets and score points while trying their hand at different carnival games. The ride can be a bit jerky for small children.

TIP The FASTPASS line for Toy Story Mania! is quite long when the park opens and it is easy to confuse this line with the attraction's stand-by line. FASTPASSes are often completely distributed early in the day.

Voyage of the Little Mermaid (Animation Courtyard). Fans of *The Little Mermaid* will enjoy this popular show that brings you under the sea into Ariel's world. Live performers and puppets retell this story with the help of well-known songs such as "Under the Sea" and "Poor Unfortunate Souls." Ursula can be intense and frightening for young preschoolers or sensitive children; the theatre is quite dark for portions of the show. Parental discretion is advised.

Animal Kingdom

The Boneyard (DinoLand U.S.A). This large playground is one that your little ones will enjoy exploring. There are slides and tunnels on this multi-level structure along with a large, shaded sandbox where kids can dig for "fossils" and other fun finds. I recommend having more than one adult monitoring your kids in this complex area with its multiple, interconnected stairs and slides; it is easy to temporarily lose sight of children.

Fossil Fun Games (DinoLand U.S.A). This small, dinosaur-themed area within Animal Kingdom is designed for children and features games of chance. It reminds me of the classic boardwalk games I enjoyed as a child. There is a separate charge for these amusements.

Festival of the Lion King (Camp Minnie-Mickey). This exciting, whimsical stage show is one of the best at Walt Disney World. It features songs, dance, acrobatics, and some audience participation. Consider seeing the first show of the day to avoid some of the very long lines. This production takes place in a darkened theater and can be very loud at times.

Finding Nemo–The Musical (DinoLand U.S.A). This is a very popular dramatic Animal Kingdom musical that transports you under the seas with creative sets and lighting. Talented performers sing while bringing puppets to life during this artistic 40-minute show that will entertain the entire family. Plan on arriving early for the best seats.

TIP A dining package for Finding Nemo–The Musical is offered in conjunction with the Tusker House restaurant. Guests who eat between 1:00 and 1:40 p.m. will have reserved seating at the 3:15 p.m. show with no additional charge. Guests dining between 1:50 and 2:45 p.m. receive passes to the 4:45 p.m. show. Disney still asks you to arrive 30 minutes in advance of the show. Remind your server that you are interested in reserved seating for the afternoon show.

Flights of Wonder (Asia). This lesser known attraction is a must-see for my family. Featuring the natural behaviors of birds, it is as fascinating as it is informative. The birds are stunning and bring a greater appreciation of our feathered friends. Toddlers may have difficulty maintaining their attention throughout this show.

Kilimanjaro Safaris (Africa). Your family will be treated to a "two-week African safari," exploring the savannah in the ride vehicle, complete with tour guide. Animals appear to be free to roam in a natural environment. Every ride will differ depending on the time of day, weather, and activity levels of the animals. Your knowledgeable guide will call your attention to and educate you a bit about the different animals your safari group encounters on this bumpy (even jarring) trip.

Maharajah Jungle Trek (Asia). Most young children enjoy animals and my kids are no different. This walk allows you to enjoy the native wildlife of Asia at your own pace. Experience tigers, bats, tropical birds, and more on this trek.

Oasis Exhibits (Oasis). This beautiful area just inside the Animal Kingdom entrance contains exotic animals and colorful birds. Take some time during the day to enjoy this spot.

Pangani Forest Exploration Trail (Africa). This wonderful walking trail will introduce you to the animals of Africa. You'll see beautiful birds; meerkats; and my personal favorite, the gorillas. You are able to linger at your favorites and skip any areas that do not interest your family on this self-guided tour.

Rafiki's Planet Watch (Rafiki's Planet Watch). A short train ride will take you to this research and education area that teaches park guests about the care and feeding of the Animal Kingdom animals and current conservation efforts. The real gem here for small children is the Affection Section, where visitors are able to pet the animals.

TriceraTop Spin (DinoLand U.S.A.). Park guests board colorful and friendly prehistoric creatures and fly in a circle while controlling their ride vehicle's height with a lever. It's a favorite of small children.

Lil' Daredevils

What to do if you have a thrill-seeker in your midst? Disney World has you covered. If your older preschooler meets the height requirement, you might try some of these rides that kick the thrills up a notch but are not too scary in theming. Be cautioned that these rides are generally more "physical" and your little ones may be tossed around a bit. Always take your child's personality into account – these rides are not for the faint of heart.

Magic Kingdom

Big Thunder Mountain Railroad (Frontierland).
Hold on to your hats as you race through an old gold-mining
town on a runaway train. You'll experience speed and tight turns
but no loops. With trains named I.B. Hearty, I.M. Brave, I.M.
Fearless, U.B. Bold, U.R. Courageous, and U.R. Daring, your
little ones may have to screw up their courage.

Splash Mountain (Frontierland). This water flume-
style ride transports guests into the story of Br'er Rabbit from
Song of the South. The ride is rich in detail but can be hard to
appreciate as you anxiously await the 5-story drop at the end of
the ride – you may get very wet! To keep you guessing, you'll
experience a few smaller dips and drops before the main event.

TIP   Place important items, such as wallets and cell phones,
in a small zip lock bag to prevent them from getting
wet on water rides.

Epcot

Soarin' (The Land). Experience the adrenaline rush and
sense of freedom as you hang glide over some of the West's
most iconic landscapes on this very realistic attraction. As your
hang glider dips precariously close to the water, you'll find
yourself lifting your feet even as you inhale the scents of pine
trees during your flight.

Test Track (Test Track). Buckle up for a bumpy ride
with jarring starts and stops as you put a car through its paces on
the test course. This ride is a lot of fun as you test out the vehicle
in extreme temperatures, with and without anti-lock brakes, and

on different road surfaces. Lastly, you open the car up on the speed portion of the course.

Animal Kingdom

! ⏰ **Kali River Rapids** (Asia). If your kids don't mind getting drenched (and they will), Kali River Rapids may be the ride for them on a hot Florida day. This white-water ride will send your raft spinning and racing down the river. Large plastic garbage bags with head and arm holes cut out may keep you drier.

Fun for the Whole Family

So, you're visiting Walt Disney World with a little one in tow, but you also need to keep your older children happy. After all, your nine-year-old isn't exactly thrilled with the prospect of the Country Bear Jamboree. Each park has attractions that will appeal to older grade-school children while being mild enough for your preschooler. Below are your best bets.

 These rides are more intense than many preschoolers may be comfortable with. Refer to "Lil Daredevils."

Magic Kingdom

⚡ Big Thunder Mountain Railroad (Frontierland)
⚡ Splash Mountain (Frontierland)
Buzz Lightyear's Space Ranger Spin (Tomorrowland)
Captain Jack Sparrow's Pirate Tutorial (Adventureland)
Jungle Cruise (Adventureland)
Mad Tea Party (Fantasyland)
Mickey's PhilharMagic (Fantasyland)
Monsters, Inc. Laugh Floor (Tomorrowland)

Tom Sawyer Island (Frontierland)
Tomorrowland Speedway (Tomorrowland)
Tomorrowland Transit Authority PeopleMover (Tomorrowland)
Town Square Theater (Main Street, U.S.A.)
Walt Disney World Railroad (Main Street, U.S.A.; Frontierland)

Epcot

The Circle of Life (The Land)
Innoventions East and West (Innoventions East and West)
Kim Possible World Showcase Adventure (World Showcase)
Maelstrom (World Showcase; Norway)
🌀   Soarin' (The Land)
Spaceship Earth (Spaceship Earth)
🌀   Test Track (Test Track)
Turtle Talk with Crush (The Seas with Nemo & Friends)

Hollywood Studios

The American Idol Experience (Echo Lake)
Beauty and the Beast (Sunset Boulevard)
Indiana Jones Epic Stunt Spectacular! (Echo Lake)
Jedi Training Academy (Echo Lake)
Lights, Motors, Action! Extreme Stunt Show (Streets of America)
Muppet Vision 3D (Streets of America)
Toy Story Mania! (Pixar Place)

Animal Kingdom

Festival of the Lion King (Camp Minnie-Mickey)
Finding Nemo-The Musical (DinoLand U.S.A.)
Flights of Wonder (Asia)
🌀   Kali River Rapids (Asia)

Kilimanjaro Safaris (Africa)
Maharajah Jungle Trek (Asia)
Pangani Forest Exploration Trail (Africa)

Heed the Warnings

The Walt Disney World attractions offer comprehensive signage describing instances in which guests should not ride the attraction; the signage includes attraction features that may scare guests. Some of these attractions are highly enjoyable and appear harmless enough but it's best to heed the warnings, especially with small kids.

Below is a list of attractions that may frighten small children. Your judgment as a parent should always be exercised. What does not scare one child may scare another.

Magic Kingdom

Astro Orbiter (Tomorrowland). The total height from the ground when in motion is more than 50 feet.
The Haunted Mansion (Liberty Square). Takes place in the dark and has spooky elements.
Pirates of the Caribbean (Adventureland). Dark ride with some scary elements such as a watery image in the mist and skeletons.
Snow White's Scary Adventure (Fantasyland). The Wicked Witch is a prevalent character throughout the ride.
Stitch's Great Escape! (Tomorrowland). Takes place in the dark and has scary elements; there is a shoulder restraint.

Epcot

Captain EO (Imagination!). The Supreme Leader is a scary being.

Ellen's Energy Adventure (Universe of Energy). This approximately 45-minute attraction takes place in a darkened theater with realistic looking and sounding dinosaurs.

Hollywood Studios

Studio Backlot Tour (Streets of America). This long attraction features special effects such as explosions.
The Great Movie Ride (Hollywood Boulevard). A gangster scene with gunfire and another from *Alien* may scare kids.
Sounds Dangerous–Starring Drew Carey (Echo Lake). There is complete darkness for much of the show.
Star Tours II (Echo Lake). This simulator ride can be intense for little ones with its loud soundtrack and movement. Try the Jedi Training Academy instead.
The Twilight Zone Tower of Terror™ (Sunset Boulevard). This ride has the feeling of free fall, eerie elements, and darkness.

Animal Kingdom

DINOSAUR (DinoLand U.S.A). DINOSAUR is very loud, intense, and has realistic-looking dinosaurs.
It's Tough to be a Bug! (Discovery Island). Fake bees and spiders appear unexpectedly in this 3-D attraction.

 Children may feel more secure using a small flashlight or using the backlight on a cell phone in dark attractions as long as the light does not shine in other guests' eyes or interfere with the attraction in any way.

Attraction Height Requirements

Magic Kingdom

The Barnstormer (Fantasyland); 35 inches
Big Thunder Mountain Railroad (Frontierland); 40 inches
Space Mountain (Tomorrowland); 44 inches
Splash Mountain (Frontierland); 40 inches
Stitch's Great Escape! (Tomorrowland); 40 inches
Tomorrowland Speedway (Tomorrowland); 32 inches or 54 inches (to ride alone)

Epcot

Mission: SPACE (Mission: SPACE); 44 inches
Soarin' (The Land); 40 inches
Test Track (Test Track); 40 inches

Hollywood Studios

Rock 'n' Roller Coaster® Starring Aerosmith (Sunset Boulevard); 48 inches
Star Tours II (Echo Lake); 40 inches
The Twilight Zone Tower of Terror (Sunset Boulevard); 40 inches

Animal Kingdom

DINOSAUR (DinoLand U.S.A); 40 inches
Expedition Everest (Asia); 44 inches
Kali River Rapids (Asia); 38 inches
Primeval Whirl (DinoLand U.S.A.); 48 inches

Taking a Break

After a couple of hours at the theme parks with small children, sometimes a break is in order. Try these favorites.

Magic Kingdom

Casey Jr. Roundhouse (Fantasyland). Enjoy a new wet play area that will be part of the New Fantasyland, opening in phases beginning in 2012.

Country Bear Jamboree (Frontierland). Take a break from the sun in this air-conditioned theater.

Liberty Square Riverboat (Liberty Square). Slow things down on this riverboat ride narrated by Mark Twain and the boat's captain.

Main Street Vehicles (Main Street, U.S.A.). Take a ride in an old-fashioned vehicle.

Mickey's PhilharMagic (Fantasyland). This delightfully entertaining 4-D film takes place in an air-conditioned theater.

Scuttle's Scavenger Hunt (Fantasyland). Look for treasures from the human world in this interactive scavenger hunt. Coming in 2012/2013.

Tomorrowland Transit Authority PeopleMover (Tomorrowland). Don't miss this zippy, shaded ride.

Walt Disney World Railroad (Frontierland; Main Street U.S.A.). There's nothing like a train ride to relax and recharge.

Epcot

Advanced Training Lab (Mission: SPACE). Small kids can let off some steam in this crawl area.

Club Cool (near Innoventions West). Stop at this refreshing area to sample complimentary beverages from around the world.

Gran Fiesta Tour Starring the Three Caballeros (Mexico Pavilion). This slow-moving indoor boat ride celebrates Mexico.
Fountain of Nations (Future World). It is mesmerizing to watch this fountain's well-choreographed sprays dance to the music.
ImageWorks (Imagination!). The hands-on activities are ideal to let kids explore and stretch their legs.
Jumping Fountains (Future World). Cool off at these wet play areas.
Living with the Land (The Land). This is an informative boat ride.
The Seas with Nemo & Friends (The Seas with Nemo & Friends). Relax and explore the amazing aquarium at your own pace.
World Showcase Players (World Showcase). Enjoy a street show by these talented performers. Check the Times Guide for show times.

Hollywood Studios

Beauty and the Beast (Sunset Boulevard). Enjoy this elaborate stage show.
"Honey, I Shrunk the Kids" Movie Set Adventure (Streets of America). This whimsical play area is a family favorite.
Disney Junior-Live on Stage! (Animation Courtyard). Unwind in this entertaining show's air-conditioned theater.

Animal Kingdom

The Boneyard (DinoLand U.S.A.). Run and explore in this interactive play area. The shaded dig site is especially enjoyable for small children.
Discovery Island Trails (Discovery Island). Explore and enjoy some unique animals here.
Flights of Wonder (Asia). This amazing bird show is relaxing.

Oasis Exhibits (Oasis). Take a few minutes to discover some beautiful animals.

Rafiki's Planet Watch (Rafiki's Planet Watch). This is an enjoyable, educational area with a petting zoo.

 Relax and Go at Your Child's Pace. Your child may be more enthralled with what might be considered a minor distraction at Disney World rather than major attractions. It's so tempting to want to rush children through these areas in search of the big attractions but letting them explore at their own pace often means a more memorable trip.

 Take a Rest Day. Typically, people think of the theme parks when they think of Walt Disney World; however, it offers much more. If you have an extra day in your vacation, consider a relaxation day. Avoid the theme parks, sleep late, have a leisurely breakfast, and spend your day enjoying Downtown Disney, your resort pool, or one of the many other recreational activities the Walt Disney World Resort offers.

6   Hidden Activities

Disney is masterful at creating a vacation destination that can be enjoyed by visitors of all ages, whether they are toddlers on their first trip or grandparents celebrating their 50th wedding anniversary. Disney offers a diverse complement of shows, attractions, and other entertainment. However, small children can be very unpredictable – they may quickly tire of an activity or be scared of an attraction for an unknown reason. Also, young children are limited in the number of attractions they can enjoy because of height requirements. Here is a list of activities at Walt Disney World that are not true attractions in the classic sense; these activities are fun for preschoolers and can help round out your Disney World vacation.

Throughout the "World"

Build a Light Saber. The Force is strong with your little *Star Wars* fan. Young Padawans can build a custom light saber for about $22; a double light saber will set you back about $25. Star Traders in Magic Kingdom's Tomorrowland, the gift shop at the Star Tours II attraction in Hollywood Studios, and Once Upon a Toy in Downtown Disney offer this out-of-this-world souvenir.

Caricatures, Temporary Tattoos, Hair Wraps, and Face Painting. Many of the Disney resorts and theme parks offer one or more of these child-friendly activities for a fee.

Hidden Mickeys. A favorite, free Disney pastime is finding Hidden Mickeys, the Mickey Mouse heads that Disney Imagineers have concealed in Disney World details such as rock formations, carpets, etc. Make a game of it and your kids will delight in discovering a Hidden Mickey.

 Steve Barrett, author of the "Hidden Mickeys" book, has a WDW Hidden Mickeys iPhone app.

Look Up, Down, and All Around. Most guests don't notice the incredible level of detail in the attraction queues, restaurants, outdoor spaces, and even merchandise stores. It is difficult to pay attention to it all when you have places to be and attractions to experience. However, you'll be in for a real treat if you slow down a little and take in the theming above, below, and everywhere in between.

Pick a Pearl. Choose your perfect oyster and a Cast Member in Epcot's Japan Pavilion will open it to reveal the pearl. In addition to the $16 cost to pick the pearl, you may purchase a setting and have the pearl set. There are also pick a pearl locations in Downtown Disney near Captain Jack's Marina and on the Boardwalk's waterfront by the Yacht and Beach Club resorts.

Pin Trading. Pin trading is a Disney phenomenon that many parkgoers enjoy. You'll need a starter group of pins and a lanyard if you wish. Once you have some pins of your own, approach a Disney Cast Member wearing a pin-trading lanyard and trade one of your pins for one the Cast Member is wearing. There are some pins that may be traded exclusively with children ages 3-12; look for Cast Members wearing a green lanyard.

Starter pin sets can be expensive when purchased from Disney. For a more economical start, consider purchasing Disney pins on eBay.

Postcards. With the ability to connect with family and friends instantly using email, texts, Facebook, and Twitter, it's no wonder postcards are considered "snail mail." Still, even in today's world, it is fun to choose, send, and receive these personal vacation greetings. Your children could even select a favorite postcard and mail it to themselves as an inexpensive souvenir. Every Walt Disney World resort sells postcards and has a mailbox in the lobby. For the added fun, why not have the kids mail them in one of the theme parks?

In the Magic Kingdom, there is a mailbox outside the newsstand at the entrance, another on a lamppost in front of the fire station, and more boxes on lampposts down the length of Main Street, U.S.A. Epcot has a mailbox near Guest Relations, and the bright red one in the United Kingdom Pavilion is hard to miss. Guests hit the jackpot in Hollywood Studios with mailboxes on the lampposts lining both sides of Hollywood Boulevard. The Animal Kingdom mailbox is by Guest Relations near the park entrance.

Pressed Coins. For under a dollar, your child can use pressed coin machines located throughout the Walt Disney World Resort to transform an ordinary coin into a favorite Disney character. Be sure to have plenty of quarters and pennies on hand.

Visit www.presscoins.com for a list of current designs and Disney World pressed coin machine locations.

Resort Activities. Most resorts offer free, daily activities for kids. This often overlooked amenity is a great way to entertain your small children. The Front Desk will have a weekly schedule.

Shadow Silhouettes. Capture your preschooler's profile by purchasing a shadow silhouette. It will be a wonderful reminder of both your time at Disney World and your child's likeness when small. Silhouette artists are often available on Main Street and Liberty Square in the Magic Kingdom, in the Epcot France Pavilion, or in Downtown Disney by Earl of Sandwich. Silhouettes are $8 each and an oval frame costs $7.95.

Vinylmation Trading. The newest Disney craze, Vinylmations, may now be traded at select merchandise locations throughout the "World." Vinylmations are collectibles roughly shaped like Mickey Mouse but are not the Mouse himself. These figures are designed by talented Disney artists.

Magic Kingdom

Bibbidi Bobbidi Boutique and The Pirates League. Visit Cinderella Castle for a princess-inspired makeover, or make a stop in Adventureland for a pirate makeover and swashbuckling experience. Packages start at $50 for Bibbidi Bobbidi Boutique and $30 for The Pirates League. Refer to Chapter 8, "Recreation," for more information on these special experiences.

Casey Jr. Roundhouse (Fantasyland). A wet play area is coming to the Magic Kingdom as part of the New Fantasyland. Elephants, monkeys, and camels are expected to squirt little guests.

Jungle Cruise Tiki Gods. These statues in front of Jungle Cruise are a unique water feature. Beware as the angry Tiki Gods spit and steam.

The Laughing Place. This small, briar patch-themed play area is tucked away near the entrance to Splash Mountain and the nearby restrooms.

Main Street Vehicles. Guests often focus on the large attractions and overlook the simple enjoyment of taking a short, free ride in these vintage vehicles. The vehicles travel between the Town Square and Cinderella Castle.

PUSH. Head over to Tomorrowland and your kids will do a double take when they see a seemingly ordinary trashcan walk and talk, so to speak.

Scavenger Hunt. Cast Members sometimes hide paintbrushes throughout Tom Sawyer Island. Guests who find the paintbrushes (one per group) may be rewarded with FASTPASS tickets to Splash Mountain or Big Thunder Mountain Railroad. Before taking the raft to Tom Sawyer Island, be sure to ask the Cast Member if the paintbrushes have been hidden; paintbrushes are often discovered by the first raft of guests.

Scuttle's Scavenger Hunt. Who doesn't love a good scavenger hunt – unless it's for my son's shoes as we're running out the door for school! Near the New Fantasyland's new Ariel greeting area will be an interactive scavenger hunt; guests search for Scuttle's items from the human world. Opening in 2012/2013.

Sword in the Stone. Your kids can test their might by trying to pull the sword from the stone in front of Prince Charming Regal Carrousel.

Window Shop. Take a few minutes to stroll down Main Street, U.S.A. and appreciate the Emporium's window displays. This shopping venue's windows feature scenes from classic animated Disney movies. The best part? Many of the displays have moving parts.

Wishing Well. Cinderella's Wishing Well is tucked away in a small, beautiful, and restful area off the pathway around the right side of the castle, coming from Tomorrowland. If you make a wish with a coin, you can feel good knowing the coins in Cinderella's Wishing Well are donated to charity.

Epcot

Future World

Club Cool. If your preschooler drinks soda, check out Club Cool, located near the Fountain of Nations and next to the Fountain View Ice Cream Shop. It's a lot of fun to cool off inside this building and sample complimentary popular beverages from around the world.

Driver's License. For $5, your little one can create a photo driver's license in the Test Track gift shop.

Fountain of Nations. Future World's very large fountain "dances" to the music daily. Enjoy the show and an ice cream cone.

The Imagination Pavilion. This pavilion has an intriguing upside-down waterfall. It also has water that leaps from container to container.

Jumping Fountains. You'll have difficulty prying your children away from the jumping fountains in Epcot's Future World. Designed with your little ones in mind, there's no shortage of kids laughing and splashing as they excitedly try to catch the streams of water. Bring a swimsuit, towel, and a change of clothes. There is a water playground at the beginning of the walkway from Future World to World Showcase and another one between Innoventions East and Mission: SPACE.

Light Show. Sparkle lights are embedded in the sidewalk on either side of Spaceship Earth by Innoventions East and West. The unexpectedness of these lights at dusk and nightfall is sure to bring a smile to any child's face.

Wish You Were Here. Send an electronic "postcard" to family and friends by having your photo taken and emailed at the post-ride area of Mission: SPACE (enter through the gift shop).

World Showcase

Candy Artist. The Japan Pavilion features a truly amazing candy artist. This fascinating performer will regale your family with stories and humor while sculpting colorful animals out of molten candy.

Drums. The Outpost in Epcot's World Showcase often has sets of drums available for your kids to try.

Formal Hedge Maze. The United Kingdom Pavilion in the World Showcase has a small hedge maze that is the perfect size for preschoolers. This hidden attraction is tucked away in the back corner of the United Kingdom Pavilion near the shops.

Koi Pond. The Japan Pavilion boasts a koi pond.

Mexican Nightfall. The interior of the Mexico Pavilion is stunning and evokes the feeling of an open-air market. A mock volcano illuminates the evening sky while merchants sell their wares.

Miniature Train Village. Located in World Showcase near the Germany Pavilion, this miniature train village includes small buildings, plantings, and other surprises. Train enthusiasts will delight in watching the trains weave their way through the landscape.

String Your Own Beads. Create a truly unique Disney souvenir at the Outpost from beads that were hand rolled in Uganda from outdated, colorful Disney papers such as park maps. A bracelet is about $10.

World Showcase Passport. Older preschoolers may enjoy the Epcot World Showcase Passport. You'll need to purchase the Passport for about $10 from one of the gift shops in the World Showcase. The kit contains a World Showcase Passport, a sheet of stickers for each of the World Showcase countries, and an Epcot button. To celebrate visiting each country, your kids can update their passports with the stickers from the country's sticker sheet. If your children visit the Kidcot Fun Stop in the country, the Cast Member will sign the Passport with a personal message in that country's native language.

World Showcase Performers. Visitors of all ages will be delighted by the unique street "theater" in the World Showcase countries. Some of the best shows are the ones that coax hilarious performances out of reluctant, but good-natured, guests.

Hollywood Studios

Indiana Jones Fun. Outside the entrance to the Indiana Jones Epic Stunt Spectacular! is a goof; the well has a rope with a sign warning visitors to ~~Don't~~ Do Pull. Pull the rope and you'll hear a faraway voice from down in the well.

Misters. A large Coca Cola bottle and a disabled fire track also serve as refreshing water misters. They are located near the Studio Backlot Tour when approaching from Pixar Place. Looking for more water? If it's a hot day, try the fire hydrants near the 18th Street Subway station on the Streets of America.

Singing in the Rain Umbrella. Stand underneath this umbrella and you'll be treated to an unexpected shower no matter what the weather. The Singing in the Rain Umbrella is located on a street pole on the Streets of America near the Lights, Motors, Action! Extreme Stunt Show.

Star Tours Speeder Bike. Capture the perfect picture for your child's scrapbook with the Speeder Bike across from the Star Tours II attraction.

Animal Kingdom

Cretaceous Trail. This small area in Dinoland U.S.A. has a dinosaur that makes for a great photo op with little ones.

DiVine. Is she a woman or a vine? You'll have to look closely to spot DiVine, a performance artist who morphs into a vine that tops nine feet. She is beautiful, graceful, and fascinating as she ever so slowly winds her way through Animal Kingdom.

Dig Site. If you're looking for a respite from the sun and hustle and bustle of Animal Kingdom, the Dig Site in the Boneyard is your hidden treasure. Older kids can dig for "dinosaur bones" in what amounts to a very large sand area while little ones will love scooping and dumping sand with the pails and shovels they are sure to find in the area. The ample shade and fans make this area a winner for grownups also.

Drums. Preschoolers will love playing the tribal drums that are available at the Muziki Market soon after you enter the Africa section of the park.

Kids Discovery Club. Older preschoolers will expand their knowledge of the natural world with these six hands-on activity stations throughout the Animal Kingdom theme park. The activity centers are staffed by trained Cast Members and are marked on park maps (be sure to check the map legend). Once kids have completed the activities, which range from tracking animals using paw prints to playing paleontologist with "dinosaur bones," they will receive a stamp in their Kids Discovery Club Passport.

Monkeying Around. There is a large area for monkeys to swing near the entrance to the Kali River Rapids. If the monkeys are active, spend some time enjoying their antics.

Safari Journal. Similar to the Epcot World Showcase Passport, the Safari Journal documents your family's travels through the

Animal Kingdom lands with stickers and personal notes. The Animal Kingdom Safari Journal is available for purchase from most Animal Kingdom gift shops for about $11.

Water fun. There are some jumping fountains for kids to enjoy outside the restrooms by the Maharajah Jungle Trek.

Downtown Disney

All Aboard! Small children will enjoy this very short miniature train ride. For $2, a child and one accompanying adult may take a ride. The train is located by Summer Sands and Once Upon a Toy.

Build-A-Dino. Stop in the T-REX Café gift shop and build a dinosaur, courtesy of Build-A-Bear Workshop, for less than $25.

Captain Jack's Marina. This location features a variety of watercraft rentals.

Carousel. The carousel is a timeless classic for small kids. Downtown Disney Marketplace has a small, working carousel that may be ridden for $2. One adult rides free with a child. The carousel is located by Earl of Sandwich and 25 Days of Christmas.

Characters in Flight. Guests soar up to 400 feet in the air in this 72-foot diameter, tethered helium balloon. Weather conditions permitting, up to 30 guests at a time are taken for the approximately six-minute flight on a first-come, first-served basis. Tickets are $18 for adults and $12 for kids.

If you're unsure about how your small kids will react to heights, think about skipping this one.

Design-A-Tee. Stop in the Art of Disney store in Downtown Disney to design your own custom T-shirt for $23-30. You'll be able to select from hundreds of Disney characters when creating your personalized souvenir.

Ghirardelli. Enjoy an ice-cream treat at this deliciously decadent ice cream shop. Stop in the neighboring chocolate shop and you'll likely be rewarded with a free sample.

Goofy's Candy Company. Goofy's Candy Company is a fun, interactive experience where your kids can create their own treats ($5-9). Pick up an order form and select your "canvas"; selections include Caramel Apples, Marshmallows, Mickey Krispy Rice Treats, pretzel rods, and cookies. Then, select chocolate preferences and toppings such as peanuts, M&Ms, Oreo crumbs, and coconut. Voila! Your masterpiece will be created by the staff.

Hand Art Memories. Transform your child's handprint into a monkey, castle, spaceship, or one of many other unique designs for $16.

LEGO Imagination Center®. This large LEGO store is more than a store; it is a destination for LEGO lovers. It not only has a wide variety of LEGO sets, but also has a massive display wall of containers holding loose, colorful LEGO pieces. Children can purchase a container and fill it with their favorites. A small container will set you back $7.99 while a large costs $14.99.

Outside the store are pods filled with LEGO pieces along with a racetrack. Kids are encouraged to create their most innovative sculptures. No doubt they will have plenty of inspiration; surrounding the LEGO Imagination Center are realistic, life-size LEGO sculptures such as Buzz and Woody, and Snow White and the Seven Dwarves.

LittleMismatched. Have girls? Visit LittleMismatched and unleash their creativity. At this unique store, you can find packages of three socks that don't match, but "go." No more worries about the dryer eating socks. LittleMismatched has expanded from socks to a variety of apparel.

Once Upon a Toy. Fans of *Star Wars* and Mr. Potato Head will be in toy heaven at this store. Guests can build a light saber ($22-25) or fill a box with themed Mr. Potato Head parts to create a custom 'tater for about $21.

The Wonderful World of Gaming area offers complimentary Wii and Nintendo DS gaming stations.

Rainforest Café. Even if you don't eat at the Rainforest Café in Downtown Disney, your children will enjoy the theming outside the restaurant. The exterior of the restaurant features elephants, giraffes, waterfalls, music and more.

Ridemakerz. Be forewarned: a visit to this new Downtown Disney location doesn't come cheap (expect to spend between $50 and $100) but it is a cool experience for car enthusiasts. Similar in concept to Build-A-Bear Workshops, guests can build and customize their own free-wheel or remote-control vehicles. With more than 649 million ways to customize the cars, you're nearly guaranteed a one-of-a-kind car!

Water Fun. Much of the World has splashing fountains and other water features to delight small children. Downtown Disney is no exception. There is a small water playground between Earl of Sandwich and Once Upon a Toy. Another small water playground is located by the Wonderful World of Memories and 25 Days of Christmas.

World of Disney/Bibbidi Bobbidi Boutique. Located inside the largest Disney merchandise store you'll find anywhere, a Fairy Godmother-in-training at Bibbidi Bobbidi Boutique will make your little girl feel like royalty with a hair and makeup makeover fit for a princess. The basic package is $50. Refer to Chapter 8, "Recreation," for more information.

Disney's Boardwalk

Beaches & Cream Soda Shop. Beaches & Cream Soda Shop at Disney's Beach Club is a cute, '50s-inspired soda fountain with a working juke box where you can share an ice cream treat. Breakfast, lunch, and dinner fare is also served. Be forewarned that with the limited seating there can be quite a wait.

 For the least wait, arrive around 11 a.m., when Beaches & Cream opens for lunch, or around 4 p.m., before the dinner crowd arrives.

Mimes, Magicians, and More! The Boardwalk has free nightly entertainment that may feature a mime, magician, or a traveling piano player.

Sing-Along and Movies on the Beach. Every evening, Disney's Yacht and Beach Club projects Disney movies on a large screen set up on the beach. The movie is preceded by a campfire sing-along including marshmallows to toast. The schedule of movies for this free event is posted on the beach.

Surrey Bike Rentals. The Boardwalk, as well as many Disney resorts, offers surrey bike rentals that are great family fun. The boardwalk area is large enough to enjoy some quality time together while getting your exercise. Surrey bikes rent for $21-24 for 30 minutes. Based on your group size, you'll be able to select a two-seat or four-seat bike.

Resorts

Animal Kingdom Lodge. Visit this resort and gaze upon the animals who call the Animal Kingdom Lodge's savannah home. Animal Kingdom Lodge has many diverse and interesting activities for small children including playing African instruments, tracking wildlife, and preparing "toys" for the animals.

Polynesian Resort. Stop by Disney's Polynesian Resort for the Torch Lighting Ceremony. The torches that illuminate the pathways at night help create the relaxed, South Pacific ambiance. At 6 p.m. Tuesday through Saturday, a torch lighting ceremony takes place.

If you're lucky enough to be passing through the lobby at 3:45 p.m. on most days, you'll be treated to a hula lesson.

Wilderness Lodge. When you check in as a guest, ask to be selected as the "Flag Family" one morning during your stay. If your request is honored, your family will be taken to the roof of the Wilderness Lodge to raise the flags.

If you're at the lodge for the Magic Cookie Hour (days and times subject to change), your children can channel their inner chef and decorate their own cookie.

7 Dining

Disney provides a wide range of dining experiences for all budgets and tastes. This guide doesn't discuss the specifics of counter-service and table-service dining establishments but touches upon special dining experiences that are appropriate for preschoolers. These experiences include character dining, dinner shows, and special events such as teas. Reservations are strongly recommended and can be made through Disney Dining at 407-WDW-DINE. Guests between the ages of three and nine are considered children by Disney Dining; adults are ten years of age and older.

Dining at theme park restaurants requires park admission.

 Before selecting Walt Disney World restaurants, check out menus online at AllEars (www.allears.net) or purchase The DFB Guide to Walt Disney World Dining (www.dfbguide.com) or Magical Meals: A Guide to Affordable Dining at Walt Disney World (www.theaffordablemouse.com/disney-dining-guide).

Price Guide

$	under $15
$$	$15-25
$$$	$26-40
$$$$	$41-60
$$$$$	over $60

Disney prices vary during different seasons and are subject to change.

Disney Dining Plans

Disney offers multiple dining plans; the most common is the Standard Dining Plan. With dining plans, guests pay a daily, discounted rate for food at participating Disney restaurants. Restrictions apply; for example, alcohol and gratuities are not included and some plans do not include an appetizer. Most, though not all Disney restaurants, participate in the different Disney dining plans. The upside is knowing the cost of your food in advance. The downside to the Disney dining plans, with the exception of the Disney Quick Service Dining Plan, is that oftentimes there is more food than you can comfortably eat and you lack the ability to make spur-of-the-moment plans.

The Standard Dining Plan (daily rate; adult $51.54-53.54, child $15-16) provides one table-service meal, one counter-service meal, and one snack per person per day, in the form of credits as well as a resort refillable mug per person. You select where you wish to dine and the order in which you want to use your credits. For example, you do not need to eat at a counter-service and a table-service location every day. You might choose to eat at table-service restaurants for both lunch and dinner in a single day; the number of table-service credits you have would be reduced by two. You might choose to use three counter-service credits another day. Some restaurants or dining experiences require more than one credit for a single meal.

The Deluxe Dining Plan (daily rate; adult $85.52-89.52, child $23.79-25.79) is more costly but provides more credits and an appetizer for the table-service meal. Consider the Deluxe Dining

Plan if you are planning on multiple character dining experiences, signature dining, or dinner shows that require two table-service credits for the meal.

 TIP Signature dining restaurants feature fine food, superior service, quality, and creativity.

The Quick Service Dining Plan (daily rate; adult $35, child $12) is a good choice if your busy family prefers meals on the go. With this Disney dining plan, your family will enjoy two quick-service meals plus one snack each day of your stay as well as a resort refillable mug.

Consider your family's dining preferences (i.e., do they prefer fast food or leisurely dining?), your accommodations, and your daily touring plans before you automatically purchase a dining plan. Depending on the facilities in our accommodations (microwave/refrigerator) and our vacation plans, I know that my family will eat a number of meals in our room and it will be more cost effective and flexible to pay as I go.

Advance Dining Reservations. Disney Advance Dining Reservations (ADRs) can be considered a must, especially during peak season or when Free Dining is offered. ADRs do not guarantee a table at a particular time. They are reservations for the first available table for your party size around your ADR time. Due to the popularity of the Disney restaurants and the Disney dining plans, it can be extremely difficult to find an empty table at your sit-down restaurant of choice, let alone one without a long wait, without an ADR.

Reservations can be made by calling 407-WDW-DINE or online at the Walt Disney World website (www.disneyworld.com).

ADRs can be made 180 days in advance (180 + 10 days for on-site guests). Select restaurants and character dining experiences require a credit card to guarantee your reservation.

Character Dining

Character dining, although costly, is an effective way to guarantee one-on-one interaction with your child's favorite Disney characters. Children under the age of three are free at these character experiences. Characters move throughout the venue and stop to visit and take pictures with each table. Typically, character meals are about 90 minutes.

 If your child is unexpectedly uncomfortable with the characters, ask the server to have the characters skip your table or gently tell the character that your child needs some space and would prefer a wave instead of a hug.

If your family is using one of the Disney dining plans, character meals require one table-service credit, except for character meals at Cinderella's Royal Table, which require two table-service credits.

 Breakfast character dining is less expensive than lunch; lunch is less expensive than dinner. Also, scheduling an early character breakfast in a theme park is a great opportunity to enter the park before it opens and take some memorable pictures.

All characters are subject to change. Contact Disney Dining at 407-WDW-DINE prior to your visit to confirm the current character lineup.

Magic Kingdom

Cinderella's Royal Table (Breakfast, adult $$$$, child $$$; Lunch, adult $$$$, child $$$; Dinner, adult $$$$, child $$$). Fairytale Dining is a very popular breakfast, lunch, and dinner experience located in the Magic Kingdom's Cinderella Castle; pricing includes gratuity. Meet Cinderella in the foyer when you arrive and the moment will be captured forever by a photographer as part of the included photo package. Please note that Cinderella does not actually attend the meal; Cinderella's princess friends will dine with her guests. Currently, this meal is on Belle's, Jasmine's, and Snow White's royal calendars.

 It can be **extremely** difficult to secure a reservation at this very popular dining experience. Call Disney Dining at 407-WDW-DINE exactly 180 (up to 190 days from arrival date for on-site guests) days prior to the day you wish to dine. Begin calling a few minutes before Disney Dining opens at 7 a.m. ET or book online at 6 a.m. ET.

The Crystal Palace (Breakfast, adult $$$, child $; Lunch, adult $$$, child $$; Dinner, adult $$$$, child $$). Winnie the Pooh and other natives of the Hundred Acre Wood, including Tigger, Eyeore, and Piglet, interact with your little ones during this breakfast, lunch, and dinner buffet. This Victorian-inspired eatery is beautiful inside.

Epcot

Akershus Royal Banquet Hall (Breakfast, adult $$$, child $$; Lunch, adult $$$, child $$; Dinner, adult $$$, child $$). This princess dining experience, located in the World Showcase Norway Pavilion, is the perfect opportunity to meet a few of the Disney princesses. Offered during breakfast, lunch, and dinner, the princesses include Ariel, Belle, Cinderella, Princess Aurora (Sleeping Beauty), and Snow White. A photo package is included with the cost of the meal.

 TIP Breakfast features more familiar items than lunch or dinner; it's a good option if you have a picky eater.

Garden Grill Restaurant (Dinner, adult $$$, child $$). Located in The Land Pavilion, you can expect to meet Mickey, Pluto, and Chip and Dale during this unique family-style dinner experience – the restaurant rotates! We had some of the best character interaction at this meal. Look on your plate for some of the produce that is grown at The Land.

Hollywood Studios

Playhouse Disney's Play 'n Dine (Breakfast, adult $$$, child $$; Lunch, adult $$$, child $$). The Little Einsteins' June and Leo, Special Agent OSO, and Handy Manny will delight your children with singing and dancing at this breakfast and lunch buffet located in the Hollywood and Vine restaurant.

Animal Kingdom

Tusker House Restaurant (Breakfast, adult $$$, child $). Breakfast at Donald's Safari Breakfast Buffet is plentiful with character interaction. It features Mickey, Minnie, Goofy, Donald, Daisy, and Pluto. Like many of the character dining experiences, Donald and his friends entertain guests with singing and dancing.

Resorts

1900 Park Fare (Breakfast, adult $$, child $; Dinner, adult $$$, child $$). Located in the Grand Floridian Resort, this restaurant offers different character experiences during breakfast and dinner buffets. At the Supercalifragilistic Breakfast, you can expect Mary Poppins, Alice in Wonderland, the Mad Hatter, and Pooh. Cinderella's Happily Ever After Dinner is a Cinderella-themed meal with characters that include Cinderella, Prince Charming, and Cinderella's stepsisters and stepmother. For a hilarious character interaction, this is the one to reserve.

Cape May Café (Breakfast, adult $$$, child $$). Character dining is offered during this breakfast buffet at Disney's Beach Club Resort. Your children will be delighted by Minnie, Donald, and their host Goofy in this seaside-themed venue. Try the Mickey waffles or the hot oatmeal.

Chef Mickey (Breakfast, adult $$$, child $$; Dinner, adult $$$, child $$). Mickey and his friends Minnie, Goofy, Donald, and Pluto stop and visit with diners during this breakfast and dinner buffet at the Contemporary Resort. They might even get a party started with the help of music and your napkins.

Garden Grove (Dinner, adult $$$, child $). This character dinner is in the Walt Disney World Swan Resort, located in the Disney Boardwalk area. Featured characters include Goofy and Pluto. The menus (and pricing) rotate so if you have a preference for a type of food, be sure to ask Disney Dining which day of the week would be best.

For weekend character dining, join Goofy and Pluto for the Good Morning Character Breakfast (Breakfast, adult $$, child $). Reservations are not accepted for this character dining experience.

Ohana (Breakfast, adult $$, child $). This island-inspired breakfast is fun with Lilo and Stitch and their friends, Mickey and Pluto, during a family-style meal at this Polynesian Resort restaurant. When you're at Ohana's, you'll be treated like family.

Dinner Shows

Disney allows guests to use Disney dining plans for Category 2 and Category 3 seating at the Dinner Shows. Additionally, dining plans may be used for Category 1 seating at the 9:30 p.m. Hoop-Dee-Doo Musical Revue. Two table-service credits are required for these Dinner Shows.

Hoop-Dee-Doo Musical Revue. This boisterous, Old West show features corny humor and barbecue such as fried chicken, ribs, and baked beans, with strawberry shortcake for dessert. Singing and dancing are part of this Fort Wilderness show.

Three categories of seating are available (Category 1, adult $$$$$, child $$$; Category 2, adult $$$$, child $$$; Category 3, adult $$$$, child $$$). Category 1 seating is considered the best while Category 3 seating is the most budget-friendly.

Mickey's Backyard Barbecue (Dinner, adult $$$$, child $$$). This interactive country picnic features a barbecue buffet including chicken, ribs, and hot dogs; a country band; rope tricks; and line-dancing. Mickey, Minnie, Goofy, and Chip and Dale make an appearance at this party, located at Fort Wilderness in a large, covered, outdoor pavilion. The picnic is only offered on select nights March through December and may be cancelled due to inclement weather.

Once you arrive at Fort Wilderness via bus transportation or private car, you must take Fort Wilderness Resort transportation to the Settlement Trading Post, where the Hoop-Dee-Doo Musical Revue and Mickey's Backyard Barbecue take place. This can increase your transportation time, so plan accordingly. The boat launch from Magic Kingdom docks near the Settlement Trading Post and may be a speedier route depending on crowd levels. Be certain to check the time the last launch departs for the Magic Kingdom.

Spirit of Aloha Show. This luau at the Polynesian Resort features South Seas cuisine and entertainment including music, traditional dancing, and a fire dancer. Older preschoolers are better suited to the luau than very small children. Pricing includes tax and gratuity.

Three categories of seating are offered (Category 1, adult $$$$$, child $$$; Category 2, adult $$$$$, child $$$; Category 3, adult $$$$, child $$$).

Teas

My Disney Girl's Perfectly Princess Tea Party. This special, albeit very expensive ($265), "Tea for Two" experience is located at Disney's Grand Floridian Resort. Children must be at least three years of age to participate. This tea is hosted by Rose Petal who leads the event with stories and singing. Children can expect a visit from Princess Aurora. This dining package includes a special My Disney Girl souvenir doll, a silver bracelet, a ribbon tiara, a fresh rose, and a scrapbook.

For a more affordable tea room experience with your little ones, try the Grand Floridian's Garden View Tea

Room. The Mrs. Potts Tea ($12) is the perfect introduction to this lovely afternoon tradition for young guests with chocolate milk; a selection of tuna, peanut butter and jelly, and ham and cheese tea sandwiches; and a sweet ending.

Wonderland Tea Party. This hour-long tea party, located in Disney's Grand Floridian Resort's 1900 Park Fare, is great fun and captures the imaginative spirit of a child's tea party. Your little ones will delight in decorating their own cupcakes and enjoying the perfect tea party fare – heart-shaped sandwiches and apple "tea," also known as apple juice. To top it off, madcap Alice in Wonderland characters will lead tea party guests in silly games and storytelling. Children must be four years of age or older and potty-trained for this child-only tea. The cost is $43 (including tax) per child.

Just for Fun

Not interested in Disney's character dining but still looking for an entertaining dining experience for your kids? These Walt Disney World Resort restaurants offer a unique dining experience that can be fun for preschoolers. The theming of a couple of these eateries may be intense for some small children. Parental discretion is advised.

Pricing information is for a typical entrée or a full buffet, if applicable.

50's Prime Time Café (Lunch, adult $-$$, child $; Dinner, adult $$, child $). Roll back the clock to the 1950s and have some good ole fashioned fun, courtesy of the Cast Members at this Hollywood Studios eatery. "Aunt" will remind you to eat your veggies and mind your manners while your "cousin" will give you some good-natured ribbing. Classic shows play on the black and white televisions in "mom's" kitchen.

Biergarten Restaurant (Lunch, adult $$$, child $; Dinner, adult $$$, child $$). While Mom and Dad enjoy this German buffet in Epcot, your tiny dancers can boogie on the dance floor to traditional Oktoberfest music. You'll get to know your fellow diners as you share tables with other Disney guests.

Coral Reef Restaurant (Lunch, adult $$, child $; Dinner, adult $$-$$$, child $). This seafood restaurant boasts incredible views of Epcot's The Seas with Nemo & Friends' coral reef. Fish lovers will enjoy the fascinating marine life swimming past the restaurant's large aquarium window.

Ohana (Dinner, adult $$$, child $$). This eatery at the Polynesian Resort welcomes its guests warmly and treats dining "cousins" like family. Dinner entertainment includes singing with the children, coconut races, and hula hoops. If you're not a meat-lover, skip this one – diners are served fire-roasted meats.

Rainforest Café (Lunch, adult $$, child $; Dinner, adult $$, child $). Dine among exotic animals and foliage when you immerse yourself in the jungle atmosphere of the Rainforest Café; some elements may scare sensitive children. This restaurant has two locations at the Walt Disney World Resort – Downtown Disney and Animal Kingdom.

TIP   With an entrance to the restaurant outside the theme park, the Animal Kingdom location does not require park admission.

Sci-Fi Dine-In Theater (Lunch, adult $-$$, child $; Dinner, adult $$, child $). Located at Disney's Hollywood Studios, this restaurant simulates a 1950s drive-in theater. Diners are seated in cars and served by carhops. Movie clips of old science-fiction movies are shown on the large movie screen.

 Families with sensitive children should avoid this restaurant. Some movie clips contain large insects, "monsters," and other sci-fi elements that adults will find corny but that may be too intense for very little ones.

T-REX Café (Lunch, adult $-$$, child $; Dinner, adult $-$$, child $). This lunch and dinner restaurant in Downtown Disney's Marketplace will transport you back in time with its life-size dinosaurs, "meteor showers," and other prehistoric theming. While you wait for your table, small children can dig in the sandbox next to the entrance.

 The theming can be intense for small children. Parental discretion should be exercised based on your child's personality and fears.

 Stop by the gift shop to Build-A-Dino, by Build-A-Bear Workshop, for $15-22.

Whispering Canyon Café (Breakfast, adult $, child $; Lunch, adult $-$$, child $; Dinner, adult $$, child $). This restaurant, in Wilderness Lodge, dishes out more than barbecue with its mischievous servers, games, and sing-alongs. The hilarity will ensue when your kids ask for ketchup! Kids can be a bit unruly and they won't bother anyone!

Special Treats

Babycakes. This is a vegan bakery in the Downtown Disney Marketplace with treats you can feel good about. The delicious baked goods are vegan, kosher, egg-free, wheat-free, gluten-free, soy-free, and refined sugar-free. This hidden gem in inside the Pollo Campero restaurant which specializes in Latin cuisine.

Beaches & Cream Soda Shop. Located in the Beach Club Resort, this retro soda fountain offers both table and take-out service for ice cream. There are a limited number of tables and at times the wait can be extensive. A well-known specialty is the Kitchen Sink, which is designed to be shared by a large group. It comes in a special vessel designed like a kitchen sink and includes pound cake; cookies; vanilla, chocolate, strawberry, coffee, and mint chocolate chip ice cream; every topping offered; a whole can of whipped cream; and of course, multiple spoons.

Cookes of Dublin. Downtown Disney is home to this Irish quick-service location. If you want to indulge a bit on your trip, try the "Doh-Bar," a decadent treat of fried dough surrounding a chocolate candy bar.

Ghirardelli Soda Fountain & Chocolate Shop. Ghirardelli is located in Downtown Disney and is the perfect spot for a mid-afternoon treat or a sinful lunch of ice-cream sundaes.

Goofy's Candy Company. Although it cannot be considered a dining location, this fun store is located in Downtown Disney. You can purchase goodies, including a glacier, or build a custom treat.

McDonald's. For children who must have a Happy Meal, there is a McDonald's near the All-Star Resorts.

An Apple a Day...

I'm pleased that Walt Disney World offers a variety of healthier dining choices for children. Children's meals, which typically came with soda and french fries, now offer milk, juice, or water as a beverage. Healthy sides such as carrots, fresh fruit, or applesauce are offered as a matter of course.

Many gift shops sell Tiny Treats ($2-4), Disney-branded dry snacks such as nuts, pretzels, fruit and nut mix, and crackers.

Fresh fruit is a wonderful alternative to many of the traditional theme park snacks. Disney has fresh fruit stands throughout the parks at the following permanent locations. Additionally, almost all resort counter-service eateries have a small selection of fresh fruit.

Magic Kingdom
Aloha Isle (Adventureland)
Liberty Square Market (Liberty Square)
Main Street Bakery (Main Street, USA)

Epcot
Sunshine Seasons (The Land)

Hollywood Studios
Anaheim Produce (Sunset Ranch Market)
Peevy's Frozen Concoctions (Echo Lake)

Animal Kingdom
Drinkwallah (Asia)
Harambe Fruit Market (Africa)

Picnic

Picnic in the Park. Disney allows park guests to bring food and beverages into the parks. Although there are no designated picnic areas, packing a picnic lunch and eating on a bench or outside table can be a budget-saver. An added bonus is avoiding long lines during busy mealtime rushes.

Picnic on the Beach. Imagine your kids happily building sandcastles in the sand while you lounge nearby with a cold drink. This vision of relaxation could become a reality with a "Sand Pail" quick-service kids' meal from Hurricane Hanna's at the Yacht and Beach Club Resort or Caribbean Beach Resort's Old Port Royale Food Court. Kids' meals are served in a sand pail with a small shovel – perfect for a picnic on the beach.

Nearby Restaurantosaurus is the perfect place to pick up a sand pail meal in Animal Kingdom and then head over to the Dig Site in the Boneyard to excavate dinosaur bones.

Special Dietary Needs

Unfortunately, food allergies in children are all too common. Food allergies should not deter you from planning a trip to the most magical place on Earth. Given sufficient notice, Walt Disney World is very accommodating to guests with dietary restrictions.

 If a member of your family has severe food restrictions or multiple allergies, be sure to contact Disney Dining at 407-WDW-DINE to determine if needs can be met prior to finalizing your trip plans.

Table-service locations are best equipped to handle special dietary needs. When you make your ADRs, explain the special dietary needs of anyone in your traveling party to the Cast Member; they will be noted on your reservation. Be sure to ask for the direct phone numbers for the restaurants. You will need it in case you have to speak directly with the chefs.

At least 14 days prior to your ADR, contact Disney representatives via email (WDW.Special.Diets@disney.com) and explain in detail your special dietary needs, your contact information, and the date, time, and reservation number(s) of your ADR(s).

Once you arrive for your meal, ask to speak to the chef or manager prior to ordering. Reiterate any dietary restrictions to reduce the chance of an oversight. The chef will actually escort guests down the buffet line explaining which food is safe to eat given a particular food intolerance.

Visit www.disneyworld.disney.go.com/guest-services/special-dietary-requests/ for a list of quick-service restaurants that can accommodate guests with food allergies.

A special email account, WDW.Special.Diets@disney.com, has been set up to assist guests with special dietary needs.

8   Recreation

Recreational Activities

Bibbidi Bobbidi Boutique. Disney has deftly leveraged the popularity of spa treatments and has developed a unique and special experience for little girls, ages 3-12. After selecting their favorite hair and makeup styles, your little ones will be treated to a princess-style makeover. Girls can even select a manicure, princess outfit, and a photo package. The special girl in your life is sure to feel like pampered royalty after this unforgettable, but costly, experience. Packages range from $50 to $200.

 TIP If your package does not include a princess costume, you can bring your own. Look for discounted costumes shortly after Halloween. Locate a Disney store at www.disneystore.com or order online.

Walt Disney World has two Bibbidi Bobbidi Boutique locations. One is in the World of Disney store in Downtown Disney and the other is in the Magic Kingdom's Cinderella Castle.

Little boys will not be left out; they can enjoy the Knight package at the Magic Kingdom location with spiked hair, confetti, colored hair gel, sword, and a shield for $15.95.

Reservations must be made by calling 407-WDW-STYLE.

TIP For an affordable alternative to Bibbidi Bobbidi Boutique, visit the Harmony Barber Shop between the Car Barn and the Emporium near the park entrance in Magic Kingdom. Your kids can have their hair styled with gel and lots of pixie dust for under $10. Children's haircuts are approximately $17. Call 407-WDW-PLAY for a reservation. A credit card guarantee is required when booking.

Boating. Walt Disney World Resort offers a wide range of boating opportunities on its many waterways. If you're staying at a resort with a marina, you will be able to rent watercraft; if not, the marina at Downtown Disney offers boat rentals.

Fishing. Even preschoolers can participate in fishing at the Walt Disney World Resort. Many Disney resorts offer catch and release bass fishing. The typical two-hour excursion costs about $270 for up to five people and is guided by a Cast Member. Equipment and beverages are provided.

Call 407-WDW-BASS for more information.

Fort Wilderness and Port Orleans Riverside offer dockside fishing for under $5 per pole per 30 minutes. This fishing experience is reminiscent of simpler times with a traditional cane pole, bobber, and live bait. No reservations are required.

Horsin' Around. Fort Wilderness offers pony rides at Tri-Circle-D Farm for $5. While you're at the farm, watch a blacksmith at work or meet the horses that pull the carriages down the Magic Kingdom's Main Street, U.S.A.

Miniature Golf. Walt Disney World offers four miniature golf courses at two different locations: Fantasia Gardens and Winter Summerland.

Fantasia Gardens. These miniature golf courses are conveniently located within walking distance of the Boardwalk area, across from the Walt Disney World Swan Resort. One whimsical golf course is modeled after scenes from Disney's classic film, *Fantasia.* The second course is a miniaturized version of a true 18-hole golf course and is billed as the largest, hardest miniature golf course in the world. Unless you have a budding golf great, the latter is not ideal for small children.

Winter Summerland. These courses are part of the Disney Animal Kingdom Resort area and are located next to Blizzard Beach. They can be reached from the Blizzard Beach bus stop. Both courses feature Santa Claus; one course is themed after snow and ice while the second course features a sand and beach theme. To set the stage, Christmas music plays.

Miniature golf is $12 for adults and $10 for preschoolers.

Movie Theater. Downtown Disney hosts a large, 24-theater movie complex, which offers a dine-in option. Taking in a relaxing movie can provide the perfect downtime from the hectic pace of your Walt Disney World vacation. Tickets are $11 for adults and $8 for children ($13 / 9 for the dine-in option),

Pirate Adventure Cruise. Disney offers a pirate experience on the "high seas" for daring children. The pirate cruise is actually a pontoon boat that leaves from several docks around the Walt Disney World property. After kids are welcomed aboard and don pirate costuming, the boat takes off in search of treasure and adventure. Children are given a snack after making several stops to claim their loot during the approximately two-hour cruise.

This activity is appropriate only for older preschoolers. Children must be fully potty-trained and at least four years of age. Parents do not accompany their children.

The following Pirate Cruises are available:
Albatross Treasure Cruise (Yacht and Beach Club Resort)
Bayou Pirate Cruise (Port Orleans Riverside Resort)
Disney's Pirate Adventure (Grand Floridian Resort)
Caribbean Beach Pirate Adventure (Caribbean Beach Resort)

The cost is approximately $34 per child and reservations can be made 180 days in advance by calling 407-WDW-PLAY. Cruises run from 9:30-11:30 a.m. on select days.

The Pirates League. As the equivalent of Bibbidi Bobbidi Boutique, The Pirates League in Magic Kingdom's Adventureland is for boys and girls who want to live the pirate life. Disney's Pirate Masters will transform landlubbers into true swashbuckling buccaneers. Different packages, beginning at $30, are offered but all pirate experiences include a pirate name, makeover, and personalized pirate oath. Photos are an additional cost for the First Mate and Empress packages.

Children must be at least three years of age to participate. Call 407-WDW-CREW for reservations and more information.

Professional Portrait Service. Have your group portrait taken by a Disney Fine Art photographer during a 20-minute mini-session at Animal Kingdom Lodge, Beach Club Resort, Grand Floridian Resort, or Polynesian Resort. The $150 package includes a CD containing all final images. For enhanced images and retouched photos, book a 60-minute session with a choice of various locations. The $350 photo shoot includes a soft cover proof book. Call 407-934-4004 for more details and to make a reservation or visit www.disneyeventphotography.com.

Surrey Bike and Other Bike Rentals. Many of the resorts offer either bike rentals or surrey bike rentals which can be enjoyed by the whole family. Surrey bike rentals range from $21 to $24 for 30 minutes.

Playgrounds

There is nothing like a well-designed playground to both amuse children and allow them to burn off some energy while adults enjoy a well-deserved rest. Walt Disney World provides playgrounds at its resorts and theme parks. Keep in mind that many of these playgrounds are not traditional but are imaginative wonders – Disney style.

Magic Kingdom

Tom Sawyer Island (Frontierland). If you are looking for themed pathways with a lot of fun areas for kids to explore, you've found your Magic Kingdom playground. This island conjures up memories of a simpler time when children spent their summer days outdoors exploring the world around them.

Epcot

This park doesn't have a true playground. However, there is a climbing area, called Space Labs, for small children at the post-ride area of Future World's Mission: SPACE. Enter through the gift shop.

Hollywood Studios

"Honey, I Shrunk the Kids" Movie Set Adventure (Streets of America). This large play area "shrinks" your little ones by replicating the experience the Szalinkski children had in their backyard in the *Honey, I Shrunk the Kids* movie. Although outdated, this unique perspective is sure to delight preschoolers as they climb and slide on giant blades of grass and spider webs, and a huge roll of film. There are caves to explore, sprinkling water, a sniffing dog nose, and supersized ant replicas. Unfortunately, there are not a lot of places for adults to sit in this play area.

Animal Kingdom

The Boneyard (DinoLand U.S.A.). This archeological dig site allows children to search for dinosaur "artifacts," explore dinosaur footprints, and enjoy slides and tunnels. The large, complex, multi-level area has many slides. Enlist another adult to help watch your kids; you can stay by the slide entrances while someone else waits below at the slide exits.

Resorts

Every Walt Disney World resort has one or more playgrounds for your preschoolers.

Pools

Resort feature pools are themed; the Deluxe and Moderate Resorts offer quiet pools.

Pool hopping, the practice of using the pool at another Walt Disney World resort, is prohibited. The only exception is for

Disney Vacation Club members who enjoy some limited pool-hopping privileges.

Nightly Entertainment

Fireworks

Walt Disney World is renowned for its spectacular nighttime entertainment enjoyed by visitors of all ages. As with all fireworks displays, the fireworks at Walt Disney World can be very loud and should be avoided if your young children are scared of booming noises.

 Stop by Guest Relations and ask for a pair of **TIP** complimentary earplugs for your child.

Fantasmic! This fireworks, water, and special effects bonanza at Hollywood Studios features Mickey Mouse as the Sorcerer's Apprentice conjuring up your favorite Disney characters Things go awry when some Disney villains show up on the scene and it's up to Mickey to banish these unwelcome guests. The figurative fight between good and evil may be intense for small children. Fantasmic! does not always show nightly so check the schedule.

 Fantasmic! lunch and dinner packages are offered. The **TIP** stadium can fill quickly for this popular show and oftentimes you must get in line quite early for a seat. By purchasing the Fantasmic! dining package, you eat at one of the participating restaurants and then have reserved seating for the show. You still have to arrive at least 30 minutes early as only a section of the stadium, not a specific seat, is reserved.

IllumiNations: Reflections of Earth. I have seen Epcot's nighttime show dozens of times and never tire of the moving music, lasers, water effects, and breathtaking fireworks that narrate the evolution of civilization.

Wishes Nighttime Spectacular. Jiminy Cricket is your host for this special evening fireworks display at Magic Kingdom. It features beloved Disney characters, spectacular fireworks, and a musical score that will evoke deep emotion and remind us that we can make our wishes come true. Keep your eyes on the night sky so you will not miss a special appearance by Tinker Bell.

Fireworks Cruises. Walt Disney World offers a variety of fireworks cruises based on party size and budget. The boats allow your party to get a special, uninterrupted view of the Walt Disney World fireworks extravaganzas. These pricey excursions start around $275. Call 407-WDW-PLAY for more information and to make reservations.

TIP The child-friendly Pirates and Pals Fireworks Voyage departs from the Contemporary Resort and offers an unforgettable view of Wishes Nighttime Spectacular on select nights. Captain Hook and Mr. Smee greet guests and pose for photos. Afterward, your cruise's pirate host engages guests in song and games, and you'll have one final surprise when you return to shore. The adult rate is $54 and the children's rate is $31. Snacks and beverages will be provided.

After the Show. Walt Disney World's nightly entertainment is not to be missed. In fact, many people stay for these evening shows and leaving the park right after each show can be difficult. There are steady streams of people heading for the exits and, more than likely, there will be a line for your transportation back to the resort.

Although the attractions and restaurants are closed, the park grounds are open for quite a while after the conclusion of the entertainment. My family and I enjoy slowly strolling around the park while we wait for the crowds to thin. If our kids are sleeping in their strollers, it gives us the opportunity to have some quiet time together and unwind from the day. You won't arrive back at your resort much later than if you had left immediately after the entertainment, and you have the advantage of avoiding long lines and a sometimes crushing sea of people. Leisurely strolling gives you an opportunity to appreciate some of the Disney theming that you might be too busy to notice during the day. Be sure you exit the park before the Disney transportation stops running for the night.

 Disney transportation generally runs for approximately 60 minutes after the theme park closes. However, this is subject to change so if you have any concerns, speak with Guest Relations at the park for the latest information.

More Nighttime Fun

Movie under the Stars. Many Walt Disney World resorts offer free outdoor movies nightly by the feature pool or on the resort's beach. Showings may be seasonal so check the weekly activities guide for movie listings and times when you check-in.

Carriage and Wagon Rides. Wagon rides are offered nightly at Fort Wilderness. The 45-minute ride tours the beautiful grounds and costs $8 for riders 10+ and $5 for smaller children; reservations are not taken. Carriage rides are offered both at Fort

Wilderness and Port Orleans Riverside. Carriages comfortably fit three adults and two small children and cost $45 for 25 minutes.

 TIP For some extra holiday magic, take a 25-minute winter sleigh ride through Fort Wilderness. Sleigh rides cost $60 and run throughout December. Reservations are accepted 90 days in advance.

For reservations or more information, call 407-WDW-PLAY.

Main Street Electrical Parade. This well-executed Magic Kingdom parade takes place at night and with good reason. Classic Disney films come to life on floats covered in an enormous amount of twinkling lights. For anyone who loves Christmas lights, this parade will make you smile from the inside out.

The Magic, Memories, and You! Introduced as part of Disney's "Let the Memories Begin" campaign, Cinderella Castle becomes awash in color as it is transformed into different enchanted scenes. The "You!" part comes to life as PhotoPass images of guests making memories are projected on the castle during this one-of-a-kind show. The Magic, Memories, and You! begins fifteen minutes before Wishes.

9   Parades and Character Greetings

Parades

The parades at the Walt Disney World Resort are very well-done and enjoyed by guests of all ages. Most parades are mid-afternoon, just when my children are taking a break in our hotel room. If your child also naps mid-afternoon, you may want to adjust your schedule one day so you can experience the wonder of a Disney World parade.

 During the afternoon parades, you'll find shorter waits at popular attractions.

What fascinates me is that the afternoon parades are very different in theme and feeling. They are outstanding and will be enjoyed by your entire family. Some of the parades include park guests randomly chosen by Disney Cast Members.

Magic Kingdom

Celebrate a Dream Come True Parade. This classic afternoon parade is a tribute to Mickey Mouse and Walt Disney. It features music, dancing, floats, and well-known Disney characters such as Snow White, Alice in Wonderland, Winnie the Pooh, Mary Poppins, Cinderella, Donald Duck, Goofy, and Pluto.

Main Street Electrical Parade. This amazing nighttime parade is a treat for your senses. The floats are dazzling with up to half a million colorful lights as they wind their way through the Magic Kingdom.

Move It! Shake It! Celebrate! Street Party. Disney characters and their floats parade down Main Street, U.S.A. every day (check the Times Guide) asking, "What are you celebrating?" Your kids may even be lucky enough to dance with their favorite Disney characters as they join park guests for this street party.

Epcot

This park does not currently have a parade.

Hollywood Studios

Pixar Pals Countdown to Fun. This parade replaces Block Party Bash and features popular Pixar characters. As afternoon parades go, it pales in comparison to Celebrate a Dream Come True and Mickey's Jammin' Jungle Parade; the music and floats aren't as imaginative. However, seeing characters from their favorite movies pretty much guarantees small children will be entertained. This parade features floats with characters from *A Bug's Life, Monsters, Inc., The Incredibles, Ratatouille, Toy Story,* and *Up.*

Animal Kingdom

Mickey's Jammin' Jungle Parade. This imaginative, visually stimulating afternoon parade celebrates the spirit of the Animal Kingdom theme park. *The Lion King'*s Rafiki leads a caravan of crazy safari vehicles featuring Mickey, Minnie, Goofy, Donald, and Pluto. Joining the parade are artistic interpretations of animals such as exotic birds, elephants, and giraffes.

Resorts

Electrical Water Pageant. One of my favorite parades from my childhood is the Electrical Water Pageant. Still in existence today, illuminated watercraft sail along the lagoon that flanks the Magic Kingdom resorts. These resorts are the Contemporary Resort, the Polynesian Resort, the Grand Floridian Resort, the Wilderness Lodge, and Fort Wilderness Resort and Campground. Guests can stroll down to the resort's beach and enjoy the music and illuminated scenes of this unique show.

Character Greetings

For many young children, a trip to Disney World is all about the characters. The Walt Disney World Resort makes a wide variety of characters available throughout the day in each theme park.

There are two categories of characters – "face" characters and costumed characters. Face characters, such as Cinderella, Snow White, and Aladdin, do not wear masks and are permitted to speak; costumed characters, such as Mickey Mouse, Pluto, and Winnie the Pooh do not have their faces visible and only gesture; this, however, may be about to change. In spring 2010, Disneyland tested new technology that allowed Mickey Mouse to speak and respond to guests.

Here's how Character Greetings work. Characters are escorted to their designated Character Greeting spot by a Cast Member; a PhotoPass photographer will be present to assist in picture taking. Eager guests line up, usually with their autograph book in hand. One by one, the Disney characters will greet guests, engage in some antics, and pose for pictures. A Times Guide is available in each theme park and lists the character greeting locations and the hours characters are available.

A very popular pastime at Walt Disney World is collecting character autographs. Children enjoy asking their favorite characters for their "John Hancock." Autograph books ($7-15) are widely available for purchase throughout Walt Disney World. To save a few dollars, consider making your own.

 Be sure to bring a large, hefty pen, such as a Sharpie. With their costumed hands, the characters need a chunky pen to easily autograph the books. It will also help if the autograph book is already open when you hand it to them.

10   Child Care and Safety

Child Care

The author of this guide does not expressly recommend any of the child care services included in this guide. The child care options presented are informational only.

Children's Activity Centers

Some of the Deluxe Resorts offer what can be considered an on-site kids' club. It is a designated, themed area that provides a variety of activities, for children ages 3-12, from late afternoon to midnight. Activities include watching movies, playing computer games, arts and crafts, and puzzles. Children must be fully potty-trained. A meal and light snack are provided depending on the hours (two-hour minimum) your child is at the activity center. Rates are $11.50 per hour and reservations may be made 180 days in advance by calling 407-WDW-DINE.

The following resorts offer Children's Activity Centers:
Animal Kingdom Lodge; Simba's Clubhouse
Beach Club Resort; Sandcastle Club
Grand Floridian Resort & Spa; Mouseketeer Club
Polynesian Resort; Never Land Club
Walt Disney World Swan and Dolphin Resort; Camp Dolphin
Wilderness Lodge; Cub's Den
Yacht Club Resort; Sandcastle Club

Parents don't have to be staying at a Walt Disney World resort to make a reservation for their kids.

Child Care Services

In-room babysitting services are available at Walt Disney World and other Orlando area resorts. These babysitting services are not provided by Walt Disney World Resort. Walt Disney World Resort works with an independent company called Kid's Nite Out (www.kidsniteout.com; 407-828-0920).

Reservations for child care may be made up to 90 days in advance.

Mother's Helpers

Sometimes we all need an extra pair of hands. In addition to in-room babysitting services, Kid's Nite Out provides mother's and father's helpers. These caregivers may also accompany your family to a theme park to assist in child care. Please note that you are required to purchase the theme park admission for the caregiver. For more information, contact Kid's Nite Out.

It's a Date!

Decisions, decisions. Now that you have a babysitter, where do you go and what do you do? Here are a few of my favorite things depending on your interests, budget, and time of day.

Hit the Parks. Seeing your child's eyes shine on "it's a small world" is priceless but let's face it, it might not be exactly your speed. Although you can use Rider Swap to experience the more thrilling rides, having a babysitter might be just the opportunity to take in some attractions that your little ones can't enjoy such as Expedition Everest, Rock 'n' Roller Coaster, and Tower of Terror.

Adults Only. No Kids Allowed. While the kids are having fun with a babysitter, indulge in some of the adult-focused recreation Disney World offers. Try an evening of Cirque du Soleil (tickets start at $71), a ride-along at the Richard Petty Driving Experience (prices start around $100), or a massage at one of Disney World's full-service spas. Perhaps a round of golf (starting at $49) at one of the Walt Disney Resort's five course or an afternoon of shopping is more your thing.

Dinner and a Movie. Date night doesn't have to mean an expensive dinner at one of Disney's signature restaurants, although that is a great way to spend the evening. For my husband and me, a kids-free meal isn't about the food but rather the opportunity to sit and reconnect uninterrupted. After dinner, head over to Downtown Disney and catch a movie or better yet, take in the view at 400 feet above ground in Disney's tethered balloon, Characters in Flight.

Hold Hands and Stroll. From resort grounds to theme parks, Walt Disney World offers spectacular and imaginative scenery. Pick your favorite location, your beverage of choice, and immerse yourself in the magic of Walt Disney World with a leisurely stroll. It will be well worth the cost of child care.

Take a Carriage Ride. Head over to Port Orleans – Riverside, or Fort Wilderness, for a $45 carriage ride for two. Call 407-WDW-PLAY to make reservations.

Nightlife. Whether dancing, music, or wine is your thing, you can find it at Walt Disney World. The Boardwalk area is home to my personal favorite, Jellyrolls, a piano bar ($10 cover charge) with dueling pianos, as well as the Atlantic Dance Hall nightclub (no cover charge). The Atlantic Dance Hall will satisfy your desire to show off your best dance moves. Epcot's World Showcase Wine Walk is an exciting option. Pay $20 and receive a Wine Walk Passport; the bearer of the Passport is entitled to two wine samples at each of Epcot's three wine shops. Yes, that's six samples of wine. You can purchase the Passport and begin your wine walk at the wine shop in the Italy, France, or Germany Pavilions.

This is just a small sampling of the adult-oriented activities you can try at Walt Disney World. Whatever you decide to do, enjoy a night out in the "World!"

Safety

Lost Child

Being accidentally separated from your child is a terrifying experience. With the crowds and excitement of Disney, extra precautions should be taken. Below are some suggestions. For more information, contact your local law enforcement agencies for child-safety recommendations.

If your child becomes lost, contact the nearest Disney Cast Member immediately for assistance. Cast Members are well trained in handling these situations.

Dress Alike. When touring the Walt Disney World theme parks, you will often see family members all wearing the same brightly colored shirts. Doing so may help in the event of a lost child or simply make it easier for your group to stay together while working your way through the crowds.

Identify Cast Members. Early in your trip, approach a Cast Member and bring your child's attention to the special white Disney nametag that all Cast Members wear. In the event of separation, your child will be able to identify Disney staff members for help. Keep in mind the style of dress of Cast Members will vary from place to place.

Take a Picture. Take a picture of your child every morning using your digital camera or cell phone, and include your child's shoes. If your child becomes lost, it may be difficult to remember clothing details while upset and worried. The photo can accurately depict your child's appearance. Don't forget to update the picture if you purchase clothing that your child dons during the day.

Child Identification

Many local police departments and civic organizations offer free child-identification programs. The programs vary but may include fingerprinting and pictures. This information can be invaluable in an emergency.

You may also wish to place personal identification on your child. There are many options for a personal child ID.

Who's Shoes Child ID Kit™. Worn on your child's shoe, parents personalize this reusable children's ID with key identifying information. For more information, visit www.whosshoesid.com.

Safety Tattoos. These temporary tattoos can be customized by caregivers. Two companies that offer safety tattoos are Tottoos.Org (www.tottoos.org) and SafetyTat (www.safetytat.com).

Luggage Tags. A luggage tag containing identification information may be fastened to a belt loop on your child's clothing.

Dog Tags. Engraved dog tags are available from Internet websites and can be attached to shoelaces or belt loops, as long as it can be done safely. Even pet tags may be engraved and used for your child's identification.

Masking Tape and a Sharpie. Some parents prefer to affix a strip of masking tape to the inside hem of their child's shirt. Parent contact information can be written on the masking tape with a Sharpie pen.

 TIP   Engraved, Disney-themed ID tags are available for purchase at self-serve kiosks throughout Walt Disney World. Most machines are near the entrance or exit of gift shops. For a free alternative, stop by Guest Relations and a Cast Member will cheerfully provide a paper bracelet and will lend you a marker.

Child-Proofing

Even on vacation, there are some things you can do to make your lodging a little safer for your kids. Everything Walt Disney World (www.everythingwdw.blogspot.com) suggests some of these practical child-proofing ideas.

Medication Lock Box. Whenever I travel, I bring common over-the-counter medications from home as well as prescription medications. A hotel room does not always have a safe place to leave such medications where I can be assured they are out of my children's reach. I've purchased a small, plastic lockbox (www.onestepahead.com) made expressly for medications. It's lightweight and easy for adults to use, and gives me peace of mind when I travel.

Outlet Covers. Kids love to explore and what's better for that than a hotel room or rented house? Electrical outlet covers are easy to throw into your suitcase and help protect curious little ones.

Glass Sliding Doors. Hotel sliding doors that open to a balcony strike fear in my heart. In my experience, the doors are heavy but the locks are within reach of preschoolers which makes it possible for them to open the doors with some effort. Luckily, manufacturers of safety products make latches and wedges that secure yet are not permanently affixed to the door, making them ideal for travel. You may have to look further than your neighborhood baby store; look at online retailers such as One Step Ahead.

Hotel Room Doors. Last but not least are the hotel room doors themselves. If you have toddlers or suspect your child may make a run for it, you can purchase self-adhesive lever handle locks. Simply remove them when it's time to check-out.

First Aid

First aid centers are located next to the Baby Care Centers in each theme park. See Chapter 4, "Touring," for locations.

For medical situations that require more care than is appropriate for the first aid centers, guests have access to the Centra Care Urgent Care Provider. Centra Care Medical Center provides complimentary transportation (call 407-938-0650) to its urgent care center and accepts most insurance plans. The front desk at Walt Disney World resorts can also assist in arranging for a physician to visit your resort room if necessary.

Sunscreen. Don't forget the sunscreen, particularly for your little ones. The Florida sun is strong even during the cooler months. Reapply often.

11 Seasonal Events

To add to the magic, Walt Disney World celebrates seasonal events throughout the year. There's a good chance your visit will coincide with one of these extraordinary events, or you might plan your vacation to take advantage of one of them.

All Walt Disney World special events will not be covered as many are outside the scope of this guide.

Winter Holidays at Disney World. Celebrate the holidays at Walt Disney World. Holiday events start mid-November and run through early January. Dates vary every year so check with Walt Disney World when making reservations. The highlights include Mickey's Very Merry Christmas Party, Candlelight Processional, the Osborne Family Spectacle of Dancing Lights, Holidays around the World, and resort decorations.

Mickey's Very Merry Christmas Party (Magic Kingdom). This exclusive evening party takes place on select nights throughout the holiday season. Tickets are required and they tend to sell out quickly so purchase them well in advance; prices vary based on the night selected. Advance purchase tickets are approximately $57 for adults and $52 for preschoolers. During the festivities, you'll be treated to unique stage shows, singing, a special parade, a festive fireworks display, hot chocolate, cookies, and even "snow" on Main Street!

Epcot's Candlelight Processional. This free event in the open-air
American Gardens Theatre at the American Pavilion retells the
Christmas story complete with a wonderful choir, a narrator, and
glorious music. To guarantee a seat – the theater fills up very
early – consider purchasing a Candlelight Processional dining
package. This package combines dining at select Epcot
restaurants during lunch or dinner with guaranteed seating for
this awe-inspiring event.

The Candlelight Processional dining package (Lunch, adult $$$-
$$$$, child $; Dinner, adult $$$$- $$$$$, child $$-$$$) includes
an appetizer, entrée, dessert, and non-alcoholic beverage, or one
full buffet (if applicable)

The Osborne Family Spectacle of Dancing Lights (Disney's
Hollywood Studios). It is hard to adequately describe this
breathtaking event. Think of the Griswold's house in *Christmas
Vacation* and multiply it many times over. The Streets of
America are decorated with an untold amount of blinking lights.
Many are coordinated to "dance" to the music. It is by far my
favorite of the holiday events. This free event is available nightly
during the winter holiday season.

Holidays around the World (Epcot). Throughout the holiday
season, the World Showcase Pavilions share their seasonal
customs through decorations and storytelling. It is a delightful
way for your family to learn more about the holiday traditions of
other countries.

Resort Decorations. Visiting the Walt Disney World resorts
during the holiday season is a very pleasant way to spend an
afternoon. Each resort is decorated for the holidays consistent
with its theming. Resorts often have special displays such as the

full-scale gingerbread house in the Grand Floridian Resort lobby or the beautifully decorated tree in Wilderness Lodge.

 TIP Visit Downtown Disney during the Christmas season to visit with Santa.

Epcot's Flower and Garden Festival. This festival, which takes place during the spring months, is a great way to introduce your young children to Epcot. The spectacular garden arrangements and Disney-themed topiaries are reasons enough to visit. Add the multiple themed playgrounds and the butterfly tent, and this is a very family-friendly event. For the gardeners in all of us, there are free special lectures, workshops, and concerts.

Epcot's Food and Wine Festival. Epcot's Food and Wine Festival can be enjoyed for about six weeks in the fall. Epcot erects kiosks featuring food from around the world. For a few dollars, you can have a taste of another culture; samplings generally range from $3 to $6. Epcot also offers a wide variety of culinary-related events during this festival – lectures, special dining experiences, and concerts; not all are free.

Mickey's Not-So-Scary Halloween Party (Magic Kingdom). Celebrate the fun of Halloween without too much of a scare factor during select nights in the fall. Characters and guests will be dressed in their favorite costumes and children can enjoy the unique experience of trick-or-treating inside the Magic Kingdom. There is also a special parade led by the Headless Horseman and an awesome fireworks show, HalloWishes! Select attractions and food and beverage vendors are open during the party. Tickets are required and sell out quickly. Tickets are approximately $63 for adults and $58 for preschoolers; discounts are available for advance purchase. Note that individual ticket prices vary based on the selected night.

Star Wars Weekends. For four weekends in late May/early June, *Star Wars* fans attend this annual event to celebrate everything that is *Star Wars* on Friday, Saturday, and Sunday. Highlights include autographs from your favorite Star Wars stars, a Storm Trooper Pre-show, the Star Wars Motorcade Parade with characters from the entire *Star Wars* franchise, and Hyperspace Hoopla, a not-to-be-missed dance-off between *Star Wars* characters.

 If you're not interested in attending this event, consider skipping Hollywood Studios on these weekends; the park can be very hot and crowded.

12   Paying for the Magic

Walt Disney World sticker shock and the stress of paying the bill afterward can mar an otherwise perfect trip. These are some strategies for saving to pay for the trip and reducing the cost of your Walt Disney World vacation.

Saving for the Trip

Here are five small ideas that can add up to big savings for your Disney trip.

Vacation Club. This is a twist on the traditional Christmas Club. Save a little bit each month for your Disney vacation by depositing a portion of your paycheck directly into your Disney vacation fund.

Reward Yourself. You clip coupons, scour the weekend paper for the best sales, and fill out those annoying rebate forms. Reward your efforts by putting your savings into your Disney vacation fund.

Earn Rewards. If you're spending money, you should be earning rewards, right? Sign up for a rewards credit card of any kind; the Disney Rewards Visa Card is my favorite. If debit cards fit your lifestyle better, debit reward cards are gaining in popularity although their rewards are usually fewer than their credit counterparts. Disney also has a Rewards Debit Card.

Coupon Train. Join a coupon train or start your own. You'll mail your unused coupons to the next person in the train while receiving coupons that others can't use. It's a great way to get a variety of coupons, especially those that aren't in your local paper. Joining one at the DISboards (www.disboards.com) is a great way to get involved in the Disney community.

Bag It. With tax and tip, a casual lunch with co-workers adds up; this is lunch money that can buy more than a couple of Mickey bars at Disney World. Keeping that in mind makes it a little easier to bring lunch at least once a week. By doing a little prep the night before, you'll save money and eat healthier too.

Saving on the Trip

Walt Disney World vacation expenditures can be broadly categorized into travel, lodging, tickets, dining, recreation, and souvenirs. Note that many of the suggestions for saving on lodging, tickets, and dining apply to Walt Disney World packages also. See "Room Only Reservations versus Packages" in Chapter 1, "Preparing," for more information.

Some costs are fixed and well-known before the trip such as airline tickets, lodging, and car rentals. There are some that are easy to overlook such as baggage fees, room tax, gratuities at the airport and hotel, gas, and parking or transportation to and from the airport. Others are easy to underestimate such as food and beverage, souvenirs, and spur-of-the moment recreation. Unfortunately, costs that are overlooked and underestimated tend to add up quickly. After you make your best estimates for the trip, adding an error factor of 10 percent or so can help absorb any unexpected costs incurred during the trip.

Travel. Saving on travel primarily means airline travel; there's not much you can do to reduce the cost of gas or wear and tear on your vehicle if you make your Disney trip a road trip.
With airline travel, one of the first decisions you'll make is whether a discount carrier works for your family. If you choose a discount carrier, carefully consider all fees before clicking the "Purchase" button. On the Web, many discount carriers display the one-way fare versus a round-trip fare. Meals, snacks, beverages, and pre-selecting seats often carry an extra charge. One airline even charges for large carry-ons.

Regardless of which airline you select, fares are often lower during non-peak hours, such as early morning or late night, and for mid-week flights, such as on a Tuesday or Wednesday. Many airline tickets are cheaper if you stay over a Saturday night. The best bet is to check out airfares using the airlines' official sites, and sites like Kayak, Bing Travel, airfarewatchdog, and others. Play around with your travel dates before booking. What if you've already booked your Walt Disney World trip dates? If you're a family of four and can save a hundred dollars per airline ticket by extending the dates you fly by a day, you can still save money by staying at value lodging for the extra night. And, don't forget about those frequent flyer miles.

Lodging. Whether you decide on Value or Deluxe accommodations at the Walt Disney World Resort, you should only pay rack rates as a last resort; do your research. Walt Disney World has been offering some good promotions lately. For example, you may be able to add free dining to your Walt Disney World vacation package, get a couple of nights free, or a significant percentage off the rack rate for travel during specified dates. The good news is the travel dates are usually not very restrictive. So, how do you find out about these promotions?

Check out MouseSavers (www.mousesavers.com). Consider contacting an Authorized Disney Vacation Planner (aka specialized Disney travel agent) to see what offers are available. See "To Travel Agent or Not to Travel Agent," in Chapter 1, "Preparing."

Pin codes are discount codes that are customized for a particular person. Disney sends out these elusive pin codes and they are a great way to save on your trip. The problem is, it's a bit of a mystery as to how you can receive the codes. The best advice is to request a Walt Disney World vacation planning DVD from the Walt Disney World website, enter contests and create a profile at Disney.com, and even sign up for the Disney Rewards Visa Card.

Leverage what's unique about you. Discounts are often offered at certain resorts on the Walt Disney World property, such as Shades of Green and the Walt Disney World Swan and Dolphin, for members of the military, teachers, and nurses.

Ask about your memberships. When you call to book your reservation, ask about discounts for AAA members, Florida residents, or Annual Passholders. Always ask reservation specialists if there are any other promotions or discounts you qualify for.

Consider off-site lodging for savings. Off-site lodging at nearby hotels as well as renting a nearby vacation home, which comes with more space, a full kitchen to cook meals, and often a pool, can result in big savings. Check out ALL STAR Vacation Homes (www.allstarvacationhomes.com). These savings may be offset by the cost of a rental car if you are not driving to

Orlando. One last thing to remember is the theme park parking fee for off-site guests. Currently, it's $14 per day.
See Chapter 2, "Disney Lodging," for more information.

Tickets. It's tough to save a lot of money on tickets. One thing to keep in mind is that the daily price of admission decreases the more days you purchase. Purchasing a Park Hopper Option, which allows you to visit more than one theme park per day, certainly adds convenience to your trip but is not necessary with some advance planning. One exception may be during the busiest weeks of the year, such as Christmas week, where one park may be overcrowded and guests would like the option to leave midday to visit a less crowded park. In this case, tickets can be upgraded to add a Park Hopper Option during your visit.

Legitimate brokers sell discounted tickets; the small savings can add up if you purchase multiple tickets. Never purchase used tickets or tickets from eBay or Craigslist where the validity of the ticket cannot be verified.

See Chapter 1, "Preparing," for more information.

Dining. If the Disney Dining Plan suits your family, this is a great way to save money on your Walt Disney World vacation while sticking to a budget. See Chapter 7, "Dining," for more information.

Choose your dining venues carefully, from table-service restaurants to quick-service options. Some restaurants and quick-service locations offer a better value than others while some may better fit your family's preferences. AllEars (www.allears.net) has an extensive menu database where you can judge value by looking at the offerings and prices. Disney bloggers such as

Disney Food Blog (www.disneyfoodblog.com) have great insights and information, including their picks for the best restaurants and value.

Sometimes you just have to ask. Some restaurants offer discounts for Annual Passholders, Disney Vacation Club members, Disney Rewards Visa cardholders, AAA members, and more.

Your budget will take a hit if you purchase beverages and snacks in the theme parks. Bring your own snacks and beverages to the parks for significant savings. See "Other Advance Planning Tips" in Chapter 1, "Preparing," for more information.

Recreation. Unfortunately, there is not a lot you can do to reduce the cost of recreational activities such as pirate cruises and princess makeovers other than to ask if there are any membership discounts available.

Depending on your family dynamic, consider asking relatives for Disney gift cards as holiday and birthday gifts for your kids. They can be used toward some special recreational activities at Disney World. We have a large family and my kids do not really need more toys but receiving a Disney experience as a gift would be high on the wish list.

Souvenirs. You can hardly exit an attraction without walking through a gift shop at Walt Disney World. After a while, it can be tough to resist your child's pleas for the latest toy. Purchasing discounted, Disney-related toys at home will save a bundle. Surprise your little one with a new toy every so often instead of purchasing toys from the gift shops.

Bringing Home the Magic

How do you and your preschoolers recapture the magic and preserve the cherished memories created during your Disney World vacation? The possibilities are endless, bounded only by the limits of your imagination. Here are some ideas to get you started.

Budding Chefs. Food has the amazing capability to stimulate the senses and evoke powerful memories of another time and place. Pick some of your favorite Disney foods and make them at home with your kids.

Recipes can be found through an Internet search for "Disney World recipes." Additionally, try AllEars (www.allears.net) or pick up a Disney World cookbook at one of the Walt Disney World gift shops.

Not to worry if you cannot find any recipes. Bringing the magic home can be as simple as creating Mickey pancakes, Mickey ice-cream bars, or other Mickey-shaped food at home for a fun-filled treat.

Cake Pops. Kids will love being part of the latest culinary phenomenon by creating Disney-inspired cake pops. Try a Mickey head, Mike Wazowski from *Monsters, Inc.*, or even a take on Mickey's red pants with buttons. Find instructions and inspiration at www.bakerella.com.

Calendar. Relive your vacation by creating a calendar on sites such as Shutterfly or Kodak Gallery using your family's favorite Disney World photographs.

Dress-Up. Recreate the Bibbidi Bobbidi Boutique or The Pirate League experience at home for a fraction of the cost. Get creative with dress-up clothes and transform your little one into a princess or pirate. Enjoy a spot of tea with juice and finger sandwiches, or search the backyard for loot with a fun-filled treasure hunt.

Games. Give traditional preschooler games a Disney twist at a Family Game Night.

Bingo. Create Disney bingo cards featuring your favorite Disney characters, attractions, and theme parks. Create and cut out the items on your call sheet. For an added touch, print out squares printed with Mickey heads as the bingo markers.

Go Fish. Select your kids' favorite Disney attractions or characters and create playing cards. If you have a color printer and photo-editing software, manipulate your Disney photographs; otherwise, a hand-drawn image will work just as well. Enjoy a Disney-inspired game of Go Fish.

Hidden Mickeys. Finding the unmistakable Mickey head as an unexpected detail in the carpets, attraction queues, or landscaping at Disney World is delightful. Bring the same sense of wonder home and help your kids create Hidden Mickeys using common household objects. For example, create a Hidden Mickey on a table through the strategic placement of plates, saucers, and glasses. See if the rest of your family notices.

Kidcot Masks. Small kids can continue to decorate their Kidcot masks at home. Commemorate a special day by adding pictures and craft items such as ribbon and feathers to your Disney Kidcot mask, or start a new mask.

Puppet Shows. Recreate your favorite Disney World stage show, such as Finding Nemo or Festival of the Lion King, at home with puppets. Pull out your trusty craft supplies and help your kids create their own artistic interpretations of the live Disney show characters.

Add a simple backdrop and some music and then invite family and friends for a Disney-themed puppet show.

Scrapbook. Have your children select their favorite vacation photographs to make a personal Disney scrapbook. Your preschoolers can narrate your trip by providing captions for the pictures. Mom or Dad can do the writing while the little ones decorate the pages using stickers and crayons. Many craft stores sell pre-packaged Disney scrapbook kits and sticker sets. For those less crafty this is a quick and easy way to craft for all ages. The Affordable Mouse (www.theaffordablemouse.com) suggests using free memorabilia from your stay to personalize the scrapbook. Think about using park maps, theme park passes, an unused FASTPASS, Mickey "confetti," and more.

Shadowbox. Protect and display mementos of your trip by helping your kids assemble a Disney shadowbox. Your children can choose their favorite mementos – a "First Visit" button, an autograph book, an Epcot Kidcot mask, or a flower lei from the Polynesian Resort. Help your little ones to carefully arrange the reminders of their Disney World trip in the shadowbox.

Share Memories. Your family and friends will love a Disney World trip report – from your kids' perspectives. Document their thoughts about the trip with a journal or online blog. You may be surprised at what they remember as the highlight of their trip. With a journal, you can transcribe your children's words and preserve memories of each day of your trip. Your preschoolers can add drawings and other decorations. Copy these pages and bind them to send to friends and family. A private online blog is another great way to share your Disney trip – in your children's own words. As always, your child's privacy should be fiercely protected, especially online. Sites like WordPress (www.wordpress.com) allow you to create private, members-only blogs that can be accessed only by those you allow.

Use park maps, the Disney World website, and personal pictures to spark your children's memories of the trip.

Tunes. Pick up a CD of Disney theme park music in one of the Walt Disney World gift shops or order online after your visit. See how many attractions your kids remember just from listening to the music.

Zoologist. Learn more about your favorite Animal Kingdom wildlife. Use a photograph of your kids' favorite animal as the inspiration for this project. A trip to your local library or an afternoon on the Internet will answer some of your toddler's burning questions: What does the animal eat? Where does this animal live? Does this critter typically have lots of brothers and sisters? Draw a poster to describe this animal.

These are only a few ideas to get you started; with a little creativity and ingenuity, you can adapt almost all of your child's favorite activities to a Disney World theme.

Resources

Phone Numbers

Bass Fishing Excursions	407-WDW-BASS
Best Friends Pet Care	877-4-WDW-PETS
Bibbidi Bobbidi Boutique	407-WDW-STYLE
Disney Dining	407-WDW-DINE
Disney Guest Information	407-WDW-MAGIC
Disney Recreation	407-WDW-PLAY
Disney Room-Only Reservations	407-939-7429
Disney Vacation Package Booking	407-939-7675
Disney's Cake Hotline	407-827-2253
Disney's Professional Portrait Service	407-934-4004
Kid's Nite Out	407-828-0920
Lost and Found	407-824-4245
The Pirates League Reservations	407-WDW-CREW

Websites

Official Disney Website

Walt Disney World
www.disneyworld.com

Planning a Visit with Kids

Walt Disney World Moms Panel
www.disneyworldmoms.com

General Planning

AllEars.Net
www.allears.net

Disney Information Station (DIS)
www.wdwinfo.com

PassPorter
www.passporter.com

Planning with a Subscription

RideMax
www.ridemax.com

Tour Guide Mike
www.tourguidemike.com

Touring Plans
www.touringplans.com

Disney Savings

MouseSavers.com
www.mousesavers.com

Undercover Tourist
www.undercovertourist.com

Child Care

Kid's Nite Out
www.kidsniteout.com

Baby Gear Rentals

Baby's Away
www.babysaway.com

A Baby's Best Friend
www.abbf.com

Stroller Rentals

Orlando Stroller Rentals
www.orlandostrollerrentals.com

Grocery and Baby Supplies Delivery

Babies Travel Lite
www.babiestravellite.com

GardenGrocer.com
www.gardengrocer.com

JetSetBabies
www.jetsetbabies.com

WeGoShop.com
www.wegoshop.com

Books

The Complete Walt Disney World by Julie Neal and Mike Neal.

Hidden Mickeys: A Field Guide to Walt Disney World's Best-Kept Secrets by Steven M. Barrett.

The Unofficial Guide to Walt Disney World by Bob Sehlinger, Menasha Ridge, and Len Testa.

The Walt Disney World Trivia Books by Louis A. Mongello

Local Shopping and Medical Care

Grocery Stores

Publix
Xentury City Center
2925 International Drive
Kissimmee
407-397-1171

Regency Village Shopping Center
8145 Vineland Ave.
Orlando
407-238-9924

Winn-Dixie
Includes Pharmacy
11957 S. Apopka Vineland Rd.
Orlando
407-465-8600

Big-Box Stores

Target
Includes Pharmacy
Memorial Hwy.
4795 W Irlo Bronson
Kissimmee
407-594-0029

Includes Pharmacy
3200 Rolling Oaks Blvd
Kissimmee
321-677-3971

Wal-Mart Supercenter
Includes Pharmacy
3250 Vineland Rd.
Kissimmee
407-397-1125

Medical Care

After Hours Pediatrics Urgent Care
www.afterhourspediatrics.com
4101 Town Center Blvd.
Orlando
407- 850-3497

Centra Care: Florida Hospital Urgent Care
Complimentary Transportation to an Urgent Care Center
407-938-0650

Florida Hospital Celebration Health
400 Celebration Pl.
Celebration
407-303-4000

Lake Buena Vista Centra Care
Walk-In Facility
Near Downtown Disney
12500 S. Apopka Vineland Rd.
Orlando
407-934-CARE (2273)

Pharmacy

Turner Drugs
Does not accept insurance
Delivers to Walt Disney World Resort
1530 Celebration Blvd.
Celebration
407-828-8125

Religious Services

Catholic Mass

Basilica of the National Shrine of Mary, Queen of the Universe
8300 Vineland Avenue
Orlando
407-239-6600
www.maryqueenoftheuniverse.org

Corpus Christi Catholic Church
1050 Celebration Ave.
Celebration
321-939-1491
www.celebrationcatholic.org

Protestant Services

Community Presbyterian
511 Celebration Ave.
Celebration, FL 34747
407-566-1633
www.commpres.org

Jewish Services
Conservative

Southwest Orlando Jewish Congregation
11200 S. Apopka-Vineland Road
Orlando
407-239-5444
www.sojc.org

Reformed

Congregation of Reform Judaism
928 Malone Drive
Orlando, FL 32810
407-645-0444
www.crjorlando.org

Muslim Worship
There is a designated meditation area in the Morocco Pavilion's
Morocco Museum in the Epcot's World Showcase.

FASTPASS Attractions

The following attractions offer FASTPASS.

Magic Kingdom
Big Thunder Mountain Railroad
Buzz Lightyear's Space Ranger Spin
Jungle Cruise
The Many Adventures of Winnie the Pooh
Peter Pan's Flight
Space Mountain
Splash Mountain
Town Square Theater

Epcot
Captain EO
Living with the Land
Maelstrom
Mission: SPACE
Soarin'
Test Track

Hollywood Studios
Rock 'n' Roller Coaster Starring Aerosmith
Star Tours II
Toy Story Mania!
The Twilight Zone Tower of Terror
Voyage of the Little Mermaid

Animal Kingdom
DINOSAUR
Expedition Everest
Kali River Rapids
Kilimanjaro Safaris

Must-Do List

The attractions listed below are not the only ones your preschoolers will enjoy – they are simply the highlights for each age group.

When selecting attractions, parental discretion should be used and your child's personality and fears should be taken into account.

Toddlers (Ages 2-3)

Magic Kingdom
Celebrate a Dream Come True Parade
Dream Along with Mickey
Dumbo the Flying Elephant
"it's a small world"
The Many Adventures of Winnie the Pooh
Prince Charming Regal Carrousel
Town Square Theater
Walt Disney World Railroad

Epcot
Epcot Character Spot
Kidcot Fun Stops
The Seas with Nemo & Friends Ride
Turtle Talk with Crush

Hollywood Studios
Beauty and the Beast – Live on Stage
Disney Junior – Live on Stage!
"Honey, I Shrunk the Kids" Movie Set Adventure
Muppet Vision 3D

Animal Kingdom
Affection Section
Dig Site at The Boneyard
Festival of the Lion King
Maharajah Jungle Trek
Pangani Forest Exploration Trail
TriceraTop Spin

Preschoolers (Ages 4-5)

Magic Kingdom
The Barnstormer
Buzz Lightyear's Space Ranger Spin
Captain Jack Sparrow's Pirate Tutorial
Celebrate a Dream Come True Parade
Dream Along with Mickey
Magic Carpets of Aladdin
The Many Adventures of Winnie the Pooh
Mickey's PhilharMagic
Main Street Electrical Parade
Town Square Theater
Walt Disney World Railroad
Wishes Nighttime Spectacular

Epcot
Circle of Life
Epcot Character Spot

IllumiNations: Reflections of Earth
Kidcot Fun Stops
Turtle Talk with Crush

Hollywood Studios
Beauty and the Beast – Live on Stage
Disney Junior – Live on Stage!
"Honey, I Shrunk the Kids" Movie Set Adventure
Jedi Training Academy
Muppet Vision 3D
Phineas & Ferb: We're Making a Movie
Toy Story Mania!

Animal Kingdom
The Boneyard
Festival of the Lion King
Finding Nemo – The Musical
Kilimanjaro Safaris
Maharajah Jungle Trek
Mickey's Jammin' Jungle Parade
Pangani Forest Exploration Trail
TriceraTop Spin

Character Greeting Locations

Locations and characters are subject to change.

Character locations tend to change frequently and often the Times Guide is not very specific regarding characters. Stop by Guest Relations in the park to find out exactly where a particular character will be located or check Character Central (www.charactercentral.net) before you leave home.

Magic Kingdom

Agrabah Marketplace (Adventureland). Aladdin; Jasmine
Tinker Bell's Magical Nook (Adventureland). Disney Fairies
Mickey's PhilharMagic (Fantasyland). Peter Pan
Fairytale Garden (Fantasyland). Rapunzel from Tangled
Country Bear Jamboree (Frontierland). Donald Duck
Splash Mountain (Frontierland). Woody; Jessie; Goofy
Liberty Square Bridge (Liberty Square). *Princess and the Frog* characters
Town Square (Main Street, U.S.A.). Classic Disney friends
Town Square Theater (Main Street, U.S.A.) Mickey Mouse; Minnie Mouse; Disney princesses
Carousel of Progress (Tomorrowland). Buzz Lightyear; Stitch; Chip and Dale

Epcot

China Pavilion (World Showcase). *Mulan* characters

Entrance (Entrance Plaza). Daisy; Stitch
Epcot Character Spot (Across from Innoventions West).
Mickey; Minnie; Donald Duck; Goofy; Pluto
France Pavilion (World Showcase). *Beauty and the Beast*
characters; Sleeping Beauty
Germany Pavilion (World Showcase). Snow White
Innoventions West (Innoventions). Chip and Dale
Morocco Pavilion (World Showcase). Aladdin; Jasmine
Showcase Plaza (Across from Disney Traders). Duffy the
Disney Bear
United Kingdom Pavilion (World Showcase). Mary Poppins;
Pooh and Tigger; Alice in Wonderland

TIP Disney Rewards Visa cardholders can participate in an
exclusive Character Meet 'N' Greet Event at
Innoventions East. Currently, this opportunity is
offered in the afternoon but is subject to change. Visit Guest
Relations for times. Present your Disney Visa Rewards Card for
admission and a complimentary 5x7 photo with a favorite
Disney character.

Hollywood Studios

Stars of Disney Junior (Animation Courtyard). Handy Manny;
Little Einsteins
Magic of Disney Animation (Magic of Disney Animation).
THE INCREDIBLES characters; Mickey Mouse; Winnie the
Pooh
Toy Story Friends (Pixar Place). Buzz Lightyear; Woody;
Green Army Men
Sorcerer Hat Character Greeting (Sorcerer Hat). Disney
friends.

Near Backlot Tour (Streets of America). *Monsters, Inc.* characters

Near Mama Melrose's Ristorante (Streets of America). Phineas and Ferb

Luigi's Garage (Streets of America). Stars of *Cars 2*

Animal Kingdom

Africa Character Greeting Trails (Africa). King Louie; Baloo

Near TriceraTop Spin (DinoLand U.S.A.). Goofy; Pluto

Near Flame Tree Barbecue (Discovery Island). Winnie the Pooh; Tigger; Eeyore

Greeting Trails (Camp Minnie-Mickey). Mickey; Minnie; Goofy; Donald

Near Island Mercantile (Discovery Island). Lilo and Stitch

Dining and Recreation Rates

Dining

Price Guide

$	under $15
$$	$15-25
$$$	$26-40
$$$$	$41-60
$$$$$	over $60

Guests

Adult (ages 10+)
Child (ages 3-9)

Disney prices are subject to change. Always confirm current prices when making your reservations. Tax is not included. For more information, refer to Chapter 7, "Dining."

Dining Plans

Disney Quick-Service Dining (adult $35 daily, child $12 daily)
Disney Standard Dining (adult $51.54-53.54 daily, child $15-16 daily)
Disney Deluxe Dining (adult $85.52-89.52 daily, child $23.79-25.79 daily)

Child-Friendly Restaurants

50's Prime Time Café (Hollywood Studios; Lunch, adult $-$$, child $; Dinner, adult $$, child $)

Biergarten (German Pavilion, Epcot; Lunch, adult $$$, child $; Dinner, adult $$$, child $)

Coral Reef (Epcot; Lunch, adult $$, child $; Dinner, adult $$-$$$, child $)

Ohana (Polynesian Resort; Dinner, adult $$$, child, $)

Rainforest Café (Animal Kingdom and Downtown Disney; Lunch, adult $$, child $; Dinner, adult $$, child $)

Sci-Fi Dine-In Theater (Hollywood Studios; Lunch, adult $-$$, child $; Dinner, adult $$, child $)

T-REX Café (Downtown Disney; Lunch, adult $-$$, child $; Dinner, adult $-$$, child $)

Whispering Canyon Café (Wilderness Lodge; Breakfast, adult $, child $; Lunch, adult $-$$, child $; Dinner, adult $$, child $)

Character Dining

Akershus Royal Banquet Hall (Norway Pavilion, Epcot; Breakfast, adult $$$, child $$; Lunch, adult $$$, child $$; Dinner, adult $$$, child $$)

Cape May Café (Beach Club Resort; Breakfast, adult $$$, child $$)

Chef Mickey (Contemporary Resort; Breakfast, adult $$$, child $$; Dinner, adult $$$, child $$)

Cinderella's Happily Ever After Dinner (1900 Park Fare, Grand Floridian; Dinner, adult $$$, child $$)

Cinderella's Royal Table (Cinderella Castle, Magic Kingdom; Breakfast, adult $$$$, child $$$; Lunch, adult $$$$, child $$$; Dinner, adult $$$$, child $$$)

The Crystal Palace (Magic Kingdom; Breakfast, adult $$$, child $; Lunch, adult $$$, child $$; Dinner, adult $$$$, child $$)

Donald's Safari Breakfast (Tusker House, Animal Kingdom; Breakfast, adult $$$, child $)

Garden Grill Restaurant (Land Pavilion, Epcot; Dinner, adult $$$, child $$)

Garden Grove (Swan Resort; Breakfast; adult $$, child $; Dinner, adult $$$, child $)

Ohana (Polynesian Resort; Breakfast, adult $$, child $)

Playhouse Disney's Play 'n Dine (Hollywood and Vine, Hollywood Studios; Breakfast, adult $$$, child $$; Lunch, adult $$$, child $$)

Supercalifragilistic Breakfast (1900 Park Fare, Grand Floridian Resort; Breakfast, adult $$, child $)

Dinner Shows

Hoop-Dee-Doo Musical Revue (Fort Wilderness; Category 1, adult $$$$$, child $$$; Category 2, adult $$$$, child $$$; Category 3, adult $$$$, child $$$)

Mickey's Backyard Barbecue (Fort Wilderness; Dinner, adult $$$$, child $$$)

Spirit of Aloha (Polynesian Resort; Category 1, adult $$$$$, child $$$; Category 2, adult $$$$$, child $$$; Category 3, adult $$$$, child $$$)

Recreation

Disney prices are subject to change. Always confirm current prices when making your reservations. Tax is not included. For more information, refer to Chapter 8, "Recreation."

Bass Fishing. $270 for 2 hours; 407-WDW-BASS

Bibbidi Bobbidi Boutique. $50-200; 407-WDW-STYLE

Carriage Ride. $45 for 25 minutes; 407-WDW-PLAY

Characters in Flight. adult $18; child $12

Fireworks Cruise. $275 and up; 407-WDW-PLAY

Miniature Golf. adult $12; child $10

My Disney Girl's Perfectly Princess Tea Party. $265 for one adult and one child; 407-WDW-DINE

Pirate Adventure Cruise. $34; 407-WDW-PLAY

Pirates and Pals Fireworks Voyage. adult $54; child: $31; 407-WDW-PLAY

Pirates League. $30-125; 407-WDW-CREW

Professional Portrait Service. $150-350; 407-934-4004

Surrey Bike. $21-24 for 30 minutes;

Wagon Ride. adult $8, child $5; 407-WDW-PLAY

Wonderland Tea Party. $43; 407-WDW-DINE

Planning Checklist

Your Walt Disney World vacation will be more manageable with a plan. Here's a schedule that takes you through the process from start to finish.

Six+ Months Ahead
- ✓ Pick your travel dates
- ✓ Travel agent or go it alone?
- ✓ Decide where to stay and book your reservation
  - o On-site versus off-site
- ✓ Decide if you want to purchase a package
  - o Select ticket option and dining plan
- ✓ Planes, Trains, or Automobiles
  - o Decide on the best way to travel and be on the lookout for deals. Make your reservations

Six Months Ahead
- ✓ Download and review the Disney Parks Calendar
- ✓ Make Advance Dining Reservations

Three Months Ahead
- ✓ Pick recreational activities and make reservations
- ✓ Make your Disney Magical Express reservation
- ✓ Rent non-Disney strollers and baby gear

Two Months Ahead
- ✓ Purchase tickets if using a source other than Disney
- ✓ Make your rental car reservation

✓ Start picking up small magical "gifts"

✓ Get in shape with daily walks

One Month Ahead

✓ Make your list of must-do attractions/activities and download customizable maps

✓ Order Child Identification products

✓ Get your child-proofing supplies together

✓ Arrange airport transportation, if necessary

✓ Check your kids' closets; purchase clothes and shoes

✓ Hang up count-down calendar

✓ Order your Disney Rewards card

Three Weeks Ahead

✓ Watch the mail for your Magical Express tags

Two Weeks Ahead

✓ Make a detailed packing list and buy what's missing

✓ Confirm all reservations

✓ Order food to be delivered to lodging

✓ Buy or make an autograph book

One Week Ahead

✓ Prepare all documents: copies of reservations, travel itinerary, medical information, etc.

✓ Ship supplies to lodging; earlier if using a company

✓ Use Disney's online check-in for your on-site hotel

✓ Download your favorite Disney World wait time app

✓ Preorder your Disney PhotoPass CD

Days Ahead

✓ Pack

✓ Refill your prescription medication

✓ Charge all batteries

Packing List for Preschoolers

 Consider marking items with your initials or other identifying details to aid in recovery should your item find its way to Lost and Found.

Essentials
- ✓ Clothing
- ✓ Comfort items ("lovey," pacifier)
- ✓ Diaper rash cream
- ✓ Diapers (including waterproof and overnight)/Pull-Ups
- ✓ Moist wipes

Documentation
- ✓ Birth certificate/passport for children
- ✓ Emergency contact numbers
- ✓ Flight information
- ✓ Health insurance card
- ✓ Hotel information
- ✓ List of Advance Dining Reservations
- ✓ Magical Express reservation
- ✓ Medical information
    - o List of current medications
    - o Medical history information
    - o Pediatrician phone number
- ✓ Tickets
- ✓ Touring Plan

Sleeping
- ✓ Baby monitor

✓ Blanket for Pack N Play
✓ Child's pillow
✓ Nightlight

Feeding
✓ Disposable toddler utensils
✓ Sippy cups

Bathing
✓ No-slip bath mat
✓ Tear-free shampoo/kids' body wash

Toiletries
✓ Band-aids/moleskin
✓ Children's medications
✓ Nail clippers
✓ Over the door toiletry/shoe organizer
✓ Purell or other antibacterial gel
✓ Thermometer
✓ Toothbrush/toothpaste
✓ Travel packs of tissues

Touring
✓ Autograph book and Sharpie
✓ Backpack for park
✓ Beverage mixers for water
✓ Camera/camcorder
✓ "Shammy" cloth to wipe down wet benches
✓ Memory cards and chargers for electronics
✓ Ponchos
✓ Quick drying footwear
✓ Sweatshirt/sweater for air-conditioned restaurants

Outdoor Fun
- ✓ Hat
- ✓ Lip balm/ChapStick
- ✓ Swimmies/water wings
- ✓ Sunglasses
- ✓ Sunscreen
- ✓ Watershoes to protect little feet at the pool

Safety
- ✓ Baby-proofing
  - o Outlet covers
  - o Door locks
- ✓ Child ID/ID tags
- ✓ Travel-size medication lock box

Mousecellaneous
- ✓ Disney pins for pin trading
- ✓ Glow sticks/necklaces
- ✓ Non-Disney antenna ball to identify rental car
- ✓ Plastic shopping bags or diaper disposal bags (keep your hotel room smelling fresh until mousekeeping arrives)
- ✓ Small toys for travel and waiting on line
- ✓ Spare batteries for all electronics
- ✓ Zip lock bags

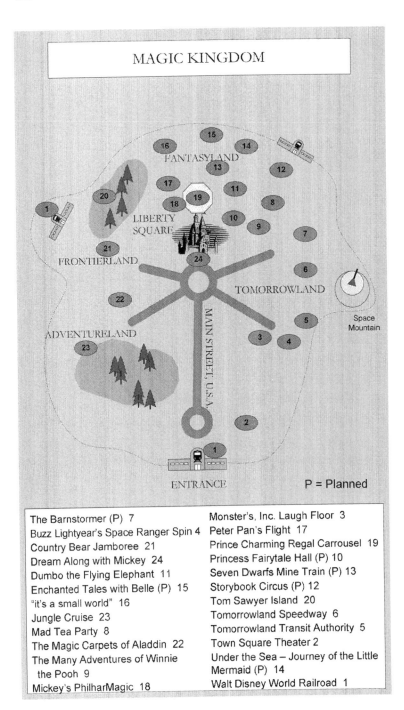

MAGIC KINGDOM

The Barnstormer (P) 7
Buzz Lightyear's Space Ranger Spin 4
Country Bear Jamboree 21
Dream Along with Mickey 24
Dumbo the Flying Elephant 11
Enchanted Tales with Belle (P) 15
"it's a small world" 16
Jungle Cruise 23
Mad Tea Party 8
The Magic Carpets of Aladdin 22
The Many Adventures of Winnie
 the Pooh 9
Mickey's PhilharMagic 18

Monster's, Inc. Laugh Floor 3
Peter Pan's Flight 17
Prince Charming Regal Carrousel 19
Princess Fairytale Hall (P) 10
Seven Dwarfs Mine Train (P) 13
Storybook Circus (P) 12
Tom Sawyer Island 20
Tomorrowland Speedway 6
Tomorrowland Transit Authority 5
Town Square Theater 2
Under the Sea – Journey of the Little
 Mermaid (P) 14
Walt Disney World Railroad 1

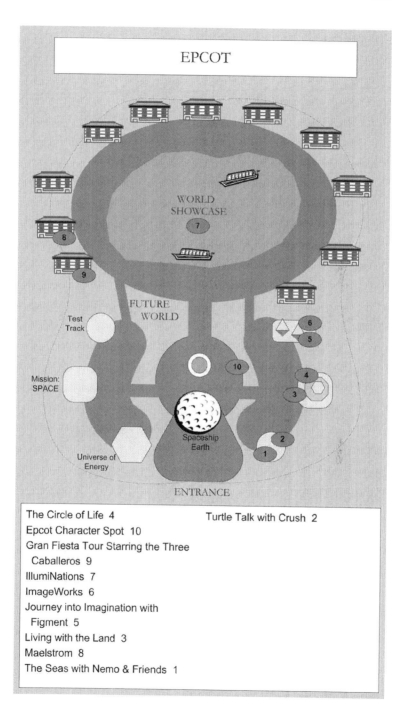

EPCOT

WORLD SHOWCASE

FUTURE WORLD

Test Track

Mission: SPACE

Universe of Energy

Spaceship Earth

ENTRANCE

The Circle of Life 4
Epcot Character Spot 10
Gran Fiesta Tour Starring the Three
 Caballeros 9
IllumiNations 7
ImageWorks 6
Journey into Imagination with
 Figment 5
Living with the Land 3
Maelstrom 8
The Seas with Nemo & Friends 1

Turtle Talk with Crush 2

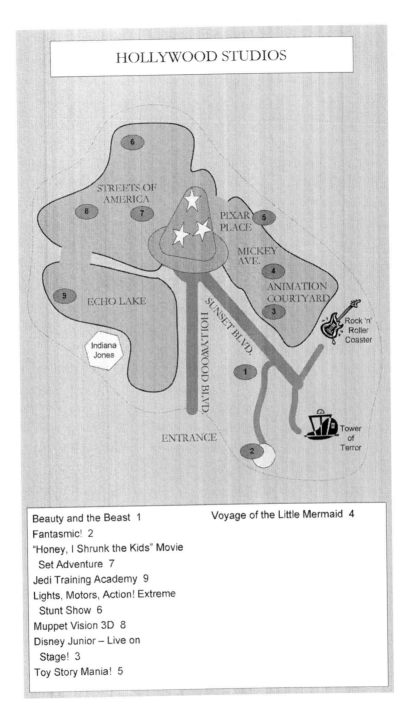

HOLLYWOOD STUDIOS

STREETS OF AMERICA

PIXAR PLACE

MICKEY AVE.

ANIMATION COURTYARD

ECHO LAKE

Indiana Jones

Rock 'n' Roller Coaster

SUNSET BLVD.

HOLLYWOOD BLVD.

ENTRANCE

Tower of Terror

Beauty and the Beast 1

Fantasmic! 2

"Honey, I Shrunk the Kids" Movie
  Set Adventure 7

Jedi Training Academy 9

Lights, Motors, Action! Extreme
  Stunt Show 6

Muppet Vision 3D 8

Disney Junior – Live on
  Stage! 3

Toy Story Mania! 5

Voyage of the Little Mermaid 4

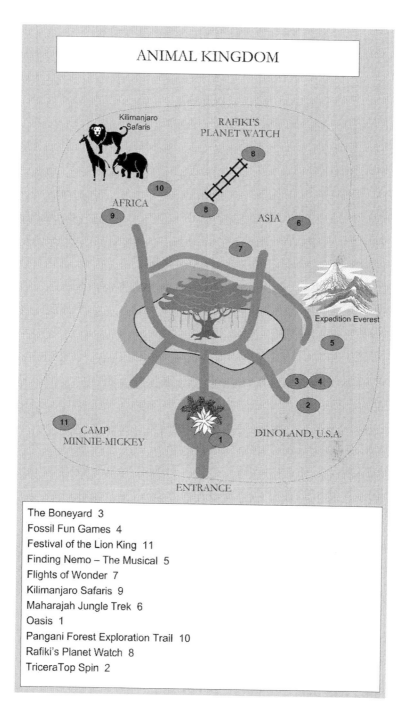

ANIMAL KINGDOM

Kilimanjaro
Safaris

RAFIKI'S
PLANET WATCH

8

10

AFRICA

8

9

ASIA

6

7

Expedition Everest

5

3 4

2

11 CAMP
MINNIE-MICKEY

1

DINOLAND, U.S.A.

ENTRANCE

The Boneyard 3
Fossil Fun Games 4
Festival of the Lion King 11
Finding Nemo – The Musical 5
Flights of Wonder 7
Kilimanjaro Safaris 9
Maharajah Jungle Trek 6
Oasis 1
Pangani Forest Exploration Trail 10
Rafiki's Planet Watch 8
TriceraTop Spin 2

Index

13296871R00116

Made in the USA
Lexington, KY
23 January 2012